FROM SEVEN HILLS TO THE SEVEN SEAS

A memoir of a boy adrift

MARK A. BRUHWILLER

BALBOA.
PRESS

A DIVISION OF HAY HOUSE

First edition 2010 previously published as 'THE LAST DOG WATCH' by Author House, U.K. (INCOMPLETE AND UNEDITED VERSION)

markbruhwiller@gmail.com
http://www.chronicsurvival.com
Interior Graphics/Art Credit: Mark Bruhwiller

Balboa Press books may be ordered through booksellers or by contacting:

Balboa Press
A Division of Hay House
1663 Liberty Drive
Bloomington, IN 47403
www.balboapress.com.au
1-(877) 407-4847

ISBN: 978-1-4525-0238-0 (sc)
ISBN: 978-1-4525-0239-7 (e)

Balboa Press rev. date: 08/29/2011

CONTENTS

PROLOGUE

The trouble with writing one's life story is the fact that one has to withstand ridicule, finger pointing, anger from those he is writing about, and litigation of course. So to put an end to these threats and worrisome particulars I will change the names to protect the guilty and the innocent alike.

I recently read Barry Humphries (Dame Edna Everage) autobiography/memoirs in which he so eloquently describes himself as having been convalescing from the long illness of youth for most of his life. Dare I also describe myself in this manner? After all, he has two decades on me; however, I can't see myself still upright and mobile at his age, so thought I should get to it now.

Oh yes, I have a story to tell, as many outside my little world do, still I wonder if they would be interesting enough to keep you turning the pages. And there appears to be many biographies and autobiographies on the shelves that continually smack of a bloody good read. Mine won't be I'm sure, unless you like to retreat to the youth of the sixties, free love, drugs, Vietnam, conscription and recruitment drives to induct children into the armed forces for twelve years; death, sex without the consequences existing today, mateship, corrupt state politicians and cops, a thriving underworld, unsafe cars, roads and motorcycles: have I forgotten something? I'm sure I have.

And back then race integration was the norm instead of the cloistered mentality practiced today among some immigrant communities. I can say here and now, most serving and ex service personnel begrudge immigrants and queue jumpers who disregard or refuse to celebrate our history, our flag, the Anzacs, Australia Day and Christmas. Stands to reason, doesn't it? Sign up to protect one's country as our forefathers have done, only to have it infiltrated by some who feel it's their right to shove their contentious posture and abject mentality down our throats.

Once there was something though: innocence, I guess.

So let me not vex you with an extended prologue, but to say some of stories I will tell you will not be all that pleasant, needless to say still need to be told. And some I have already published in a short story format, cathartic to say the least and good therapy. I suppose this is the best way to describe them.

You could probably say my story is a parallel to some of my previous writings, therefore I will try to harmonise these from past publications into *this* tome, to a degree. My fiction writing is a work still in progress though, in that I have been advised I should write about what I know: a rule-of-thumb for all budding scribblers.

Let me now explain the title of this book to you: actually, there is no reference in this book to my home town of Seven Hills where I spent the first 5 or 6 years of my life. I do remember how cold it was in this small fibro government housing community in the far west on the outer ambit of Sydney. And in the summer it was so hot we would crawl under the house and find a cool place beneath the concrete floor of the kitchen where we would play in the dirt until the sun lost its austerity.

The short stories and memoir refer to a suburb a few miles from Seven Hills after we moved into a solid brick and tile non-government home when I was approximately 7 years old. My memory was much sharper by then, as you will discover.

Seven Hills cultivated my parents resolve to improve our bereft lives: they achieved this by giving it their all.

I never achieved their eminence. I never got to thank them.

DEDICATION

I would like to dedicate this story to all the young men of the 24th intake H.M.A.S. Leeuwin, 1968, and all the good lads with whom I served. Also, to those I didn't serve with I offer a tribute, since I'm sure many would have the same, if not more revelations to disclose than myself.

2010 was the commemorative year of the first Junior Recruit drive to institute children into the armed forces fifty years ago; this recruitment initiative endured for twenty-four years until 1984. We were at war in 1968 and conscription was a response to the army's needs, so why not have an answer for the navy's requirements?

It's a fact apprentices were accepted at fifteen years, although their actual training/apprenticeship was for four or five years. In other words, they were not to see action of any kind other than training and school studies until their late teens, which by then was the average recruitment and conscription age into the services.

Our navy, being of British origins always had their own agenda and traditions, including the recruitment of youngsters to mould into the fabric required to run and maintain a tight ship, hence, the minimum twelve years' service period for junior recruits.

"Get 'em young, use 'em up and pension 'em off after twenty years," some who have served would say. After all, having served twelve years and not knowing any other life other than that of the navy, some would then volunteer for another eight years to grab their pension.

Many survived and went on the bigger and better things, along with the numerous who do in the outside world. This is dedicated mostly to those who didn't.

You see, the navy was a dogma unto itself, insofar as it would hold to its breast its crew and would not let go no matter what the circumstances, unless death, severe injury or time served transpired. Some will say this was a good thing because it turned us boys into men, and so it did, unless you had personal or mental problems, gambling and alcohol issues, relationship troubles, no family on which to rely and a myriad of other unforeseen and foreseen situations that pop up into our everyday lives for those who live in the real world. After all, the navy was your family now. And did we turn into the right type of men to survive in a civilised society? We'll see as we progress further into this narrative.

I can see the doubters pointing their fingers already; then consider this story as something out of yesteryear and in no way describes the modern navy, or the other armed forces of today, so I'm told.

Let me confirm, via a conversation with a high-ranking psychiatrist, who is now particularly well regarded within the armed forces. His clientele has consisted of non-serving navy personnel who had been ensconced within a suffocating environment and were not treated adequately for problems while serving, unlike the other services: he was adamant in his observations.

I will try and obtain additional photographs and articles from various resources, although this may be a problem if I wish to shine a light on a situation they may not agree with. Many claim now it was their *lack of duty of care* which led to the many and varied troubles of their wards in later years: no shirts required on deck, no ear muffs required while working in noisy confined spaces, no real control as to the consumption of copious amounts of duty-free booze and tobacco, working with asbestos and beryllium (a toxic carcinogenic used to coat tools that chip paint so as not to create sparks), also, we were lowered into the confined spaces of water and fuel tanks to clean and repaint them. This practice alone accounted for many traumatic occurrences when young men were overcome by toxic substances: these to name just a few of the derisions faced by junior recruits in their impressionable formative years.

It has now been realised that twenty years should be the minimum age for service in some dangerous conditions otherwise mental scarring could well be the definitive outcome. Some say early twenties or thereabouts when the brain may be fully developed, before exposure to perilous tasks including actual combat.

To sum up, let me tell you the maxim for my particular intake today: "We Survived!!"

Also, this is for my long-suffering mother and father. May they rest in peace.

Agnus Dei,
Miserere nobis,
Dona nobis pacem.

A NEW LIFE

Reproduced in part from my short story
Whirlwind (c) 2008.

It was summer 1963 in a hot land forty miles west of Sydney. I lived and breathed fresh clean air with friends from all parts of the globe whose parents had come to this land seeking work, peace, stability and a home after a war one man bestowed upon us. And now we were slowly moving towards maturity after years of bitter conflict.

One would have thought this Great War would have been the end of it, with peace to follow..........forever.

Wishful thinking.

Our parents worked and lived side by side with people who, a generation prior, and in some circumstances, had been killing each other on distant shores. Now their children were living in a new land allying with each other and defining friendships that would last a lifetime.

This new land, Australia, was innocent insofar as isolation was concerned. And isolated we were; a solitude we can only now dream of.

The fruit we now purchase at exorbitant prices once hung virginally throughout our world easily gathered and enjoyed at any time.

Our mums were our sanctuary, and the homemade produce they slaved over, although easily reaped, was enjoyed all year round. These fruits danced in the early sunshine, as did the land we walked upon, where everyone who lived there had a wide open space to settle, build, live and love far away from the pressures we now face.

We travelled unsealed roads where dust percolated our habitat during the dry spells, of which there were many, but Lord, when the rains came everything turned to mud, at the very least. At the very worst our creeks flooded, the roads became impassable, the wind furious and the damage unredeemable.

It was during one of these malicious storms that I encountered my guardian, although you may wish to disregard it as I did.......... for a while: only for a little while.

As I have said, summer 1963 and I was eleven years old, pale, almost translucent you could say, some four feet tall and four stone wringing wet, or thereabouts.

A frail blond haired little fellow who was sickly, had a stutter, and was sometimes made fun of, still ultimately accepted by his peers and their parents. I guess they felt sorry for me until I took on a tornado and lived to tell the tale. Then I became somewhat of a hero and should I say, a minor legend.

Since then I have been to war, survived countless accidents on motorbikes, cars, fights, fires and drowning. Yes, I died and was revived by a mate who had, I'm sure, a helping hand from above, since he was only a moderate swimmer himself. He said later we were both lifted out of the dam and placed on a log that just so happened to be floating by at the time. I was unconscious but my friend held onto me and made it to shore where I was revived.

Was there an old saying from one of God's Disciples, when addressing His whereabouts said, "Turn a stone and you will find my church, lift a piece of wood and you will find me?" Anyway, something like that. And there was His piece of wood and my salvation.

To continue, we here in this part of the country don't have full-blown tornados, yet in our northern regions and territory, and the far north of Western Australia thousands of miles away, we can really be set upon by monstrous weather conditions, which, while I'm delivering this tale, I might tell you I flew out of Darwin after delivering a patrol boat, during my Navy years, from a refit in Sydney.

"So what!" you say. Well, it just so happened I asked for an early flight out of the capital to return home in time for Christmas 1974. I flew out on a red-eye less than twenty-four before Cyclone Tracy hit and devastated Darwin with the loss of many lives, including crew members from boats at sea and some of those moored in the harbour.

I was twenty-two.

Was my protector there too? I now think so: no, I know so.

Anyway, back eleven years to the little eleven-year-old blond boy of my youth. Cyclones, tornados, storm, tempest, typhoon or whirlwind are those words describing unusual and annihilating weather formations that have haunted us forever. So it was this Christmas holiday season.

The weather during this particular *mean season* was exceptionally nasty throughout the state with high winds, torrential rains, hail as big as tennis balls in some areas and golf balls in most other regions.

As a matter of fact Australia suffered adverse weather conditions that season above and beyond our normal weather milieu.

THE DAY BEFORE

My friend Andrew and I were discussing what to do with our wet and wild holidays, so it was decided I would go to his place the following day with toys including soldiers, models to be assembled, and slot cars to be worked on, painted and laboured over.

While Andy's place was only a few doors away his actual home nestled down a long driveway, where upon entering the side entrance you immediately stepped into the large homely kitchen and the smell of freshly prepared Polish fare.

Attached to the side of the home, a few steps from the side entrance, was a long narrow structure consisting of a garage where

Andy's dad's pride and joy lived, a beautiful two-tone fifty-nine Holden station wagon. Connecting this section was a workshop, a playroom, which was our domain, and an outside loo. At the time we had a weekly service to remove our bodily wastes in large containers that one man could lift and carry on his broad shoulders to the waiting truck (we could not afford to connect to the new septic systems until some time later). What a job; we described these intrepidly brave souls as dunny-carters and it was a career none of us ever wished to aspire.

Attached to the end of this, almost old style country motel type building, each with its own individual door, was an under-cover area for pets including birds, dogs, guinea pigs or chickens. And from there our yards wandered off into a wooded area with a clean flowing, fresh water creek.

A wonderful childhood experience unlike anything most of us will ever behold again, but that's a story for another day.

Andy was over, as was the back and forth routine when confined for days on end to our own little world, and discussing a plan for the next couple of days if the weather didn't improve. Mum was in the background baking Anzac biscuits the old fashioned way while humming soft tunes, and still mourning the death a few weeks earlier of Jack Kennedy, who she truly loved and she even had a couple of long play records of his speeches. Jack certainly was a ladies man.

THE DAY I SHOOK HANDS WITH THE DEVIL

A calm had descended upon the land. The rain had stopped; not for long though from the look of the malevolent sky. It gazed down upon us with an intensity I will only describe now as misanthropic. What had we done to it for its cathartic austerity toward us? Maybe now it has an excuse, although back then we were all 'pretty well' innocent.

This was not Mother Nature.

Eleven a.m. after a hearty breakfast to send me on my way for the day I then packed my goods to shuttle over to Andy's.

It was calm, no wind, just an eerie stillness, nevertheless a good time to cover the three hundred yards to the homely warm kitchen of my friend's haven.

I didn't make it. About half way to my destination I became aware of...........silence. I was about to turn right to enter the driveway from the road when something caught my attention to the left. There, about a quarter of a mile off over rolling vacant land it touched down, and in my line of sight were two horses and a cow grazing around an old iron lean-to: just a simple cover for the horses and cow to seek shelter when needed.

Then came the roar of imminent destruction and with that the horses took off in a safe direction; the cow though casually looked at the devil while I looked at the cow, which in turn looked back at me. Our eyes met and his head tilted as did mine, that slightly inquisitive kind of tilt, without fear or favour: just curiosity.

The cow left the ground, likewise the iron shelter along with the barbed wire fence, and now only a hundred yards from me. I stood frozen, not in fear at all, since my mind didn't comprehend what my eyes were seeing; a thing I had never witnessed before and had only read or heard of occasionally.

It sucked me out of my rubber boots and straight up. My toys surrounded me as if they had come to life and danced around of their own accord in slow motion, then I was joined by other flotsam and jetsam while the cow mooed its disbelief a distance off.....who knew where! The danger finally dawned on me when the wire and iron roof entered the stage and pirouetted in their whirl as if at a ball.

Face down at an altitude of, I would guess now to be around a hundred feet, I circled Andy's house and witnessed fibro and tiles dismembering and racing up to meet me, all the while taking in the view and flying with still no real fear, unlike a few squawking frightened chickens soaring nearby. I'm sure it was at this point I felt protected. A gentle hand cradled me and let me watch the scene below as the tornado reeked vengeance on a small community undeserving of its wrath. Although not a huge beast its ferocity was something to behold and the damage it caused swathing through our world made headlines as it climaxed with the demolition of a small school some distance away. Luckily it was Christmas vacation.

As for me, I survived. My cherub snatched me away from the ogre's arms and placed me softly in the mud at Andy's kitchen door; in fact, so deep in the mud that I was miraculously spared when coiled barbed wire and rolled up iron roofing rolled over the top of me, then hurtled into the rear of the family station wagon while taking half the garage roof with it.

Muffled worried voices as my mum and dad came frantically searching, along with disbelieving and anxious neighbours from surrounding homes, especially Andy's parents and sister, then Andy himself, all struck dumb by the events of the last few moments. And where was I? No one knew immediately, until deep within the thick mud Andy's dad saw movement. I was dragged to the surface amidst fears for my wellbeing and raced to a sheltered warm place wrapped in blankets, where to everyone's amazement I was deemed fit and well, considering.

My parents took me home and sank me into the best bath I have ever had. Every nook and cranny was filled with mud, and I mean *every* orifice.

And not a scratch to be found.

1ˢᵗ Chapter

WINTER 1968

'Old and young, we are all on our last cruise.'

(Virginibus Puerisque)

It was early evening at Sydney's Central Station on a raw, miserable and blustery night when I first started to feel the fear of being alone, although I was in the presence of at least a hundred other lost souls, all Junior Recruits, volunteers and now guests of the Royal Australian Navy. I was fifteen years old as were most of the other children.

I say children because we were; I guess we were mostly uncontrollable in our own environment at home, but not overtly so in comparison to our youth of today. So here we were after jumping up and down wanting our parents to sign the necessary papers to let us spread out delicate wings, otherwise we would make their lives more miserable than they already were. Eventually, as we grew to know each other, all our stories seemed to articulate a common home situation, except of course the young petty criminals who were 'advised' to sign up or be institutionalised.

I had asked my parents if I could join and when they could see no alternative to cope with my wicked ways, they agreed, even though the H.M.A.S Melbourne had taken eighty two lives at sea in a mishap with H.M.A.S. Voyager, and then sunk the U.S.S. Frank E. Evans a year after I joined, with the loss of seventy four lives. In addition, I had just received my orders the very month H.M.A.S. Hobart took direct hits on the gunline in Vietnam with tragic loss of life in June 1968. My poor parents must have been tearing their hair out, especially with *both* their sons now serving.

With the Vietnam War in full swing my older brother was already in the army and only months away from being shipped to Vung Tau as a captain in audit.

Let me say here I, in no way, consider or compare myself with those poor souls who served in the 'boonies' *in country;* still, years later it was told to me in no uncertain terms that we had all signed on to protect our country in a time of war with no certainty as to how our enemies would react to *our* retaliating to *their* aggression. We were there for twelve years to defend and die if necessary. And I was not really surprised to learn also, in the same conversation, how ten to twenty per cent actually saw action, while all other personnel served in a supporting role, as did we. Nevertheless, he confirmed danger lurked everywhere for *all* those who did serve.

A story was told to me when I embarked on the Vung Tau Ferry- H.M.A.S. Sydney- the following year after I joined, of a young soldier who stepped onto a rusty nail the day after he set foot in the war zone. Within a few days he had developed septicaemia, which led to other severe health problems; finally he was sent home, only then to be granted a military pension due to ongoing medical conditions.

1968 was also a time of protests, American personnel on R and R (Rest and Recreation), drug culture, corruption, free love, of which I had been a reluctant non-participant, and the decline of European communism. Also, the invasion of Czechoslovakia, the resistance to totalitarianism in Poland, East Germany and the Soviet Union, and with communist revolutions in Cambodia and Vietnam taking a hold and shaking to hell out of the West, our governments were in a quandary. Furthermore, with the violent student demonstrations in western democracies and the assassinations of Martin Luther

King and Robert Kennedy, Richard Nixon then came to power in the United States and escalated the war in Vietnam. This was due to the Tet Offensive early in 1968, which saw the near defeat of allied forces and the takeover of the south by their northern antagonists. Sponsored by China at the time the affinity by the North Vietnamese toward their ally was not all-encompassing though, with the Vietnamese eventually disassociating themselves from China soon after our withdrawal.

John Gorton had become Prime Minister by default after, most say, the accidental drowning of the then Prime Minister, Harold Holt. Movies like Kubrick's 2001, Bonnie and Clyde and the Graduate were all the rage, while hits like Mrs Robinson, Hey Jude, Sunshine of Your Love from Cream, Born to Be Wild by Steppenwolf and the Stones Jumpin' Jack Flash topped the charts.

As for me, I was homesick four thousand miles away for Merrilee Rush's Angel of the Morning, Goldsboro's Honey, The Stone Phoneys' (I am, and always will be a fan of Linda Ronstadt) Different Drum, and Bridge Over Troubled Water first released in 1969 along with Nilsson's Everybody's Talkin' (at me). Such was my disposition, then.

Some even say 1968 was a year that changed the world, and here I was, five foot nothing and six stone wringing wet, fifteen years old and ready to defend my country: Yes, 1968 definitely changed me.

~~~~~~~~~~~~~~~~~~~

We all stood with our hands in our pockets shivering under a cheerless and dreary night sky, waiting for a train to take us away to the further most state in our great divide: to Western Australia, where, for a full year, our naval boarding school was to be our salvation, our deliverance; turning us boys into men with a variety of activities and extreme correction of our wilful young ways. Freedom from our parents clutches, free from school, homework and chores, to do as we pleased; smoke cigarettes, drink beer, travel and have sex with wild, wild women, who hadn't at that stage taken to spitting on armed forces personnel. Were we in for the surprise of our lives?

'Regimentation' would have been somewhat altruistic in describing our forthcoming adventure.

With four thousand miles to go over the next four days to collect juveniles from other states, the journey was eventful and uneventful at the same time, with a collection of eclectic do-gooders and no-hopers all corralled into old rickety cattle trucks to wile away the hours with cigarettes, smuggled grog and comic books, including *yippees*. These were cheap paperback westerns that were to include B grade western movies with which we were soon to be inundated due to their popularity at the time, along with B grade war movies referred to as *warries*.

We told dirty jokes from dawn to dusk and beyond. We talked about our friends and relatives back home and we discussed the girlfriends we had left behind. Some even had had sex, but I somehow believed these stories were somewhat exaggerated, to say the least.

While I had a girlfriend, Kerrie, to whom I had said goodbye, I told them we had not been intimate (I hadn't 'got into her pants' was the terminology, even way back then); nevertheless I did tell them of my first real encounter with a very real prostitute paid for by my school mates as a farewell present.

I jest you not. They had taken me into Kings Cross in the bad old days and onto the back streets where you could pick your own girl/woman, each of them sitting in front of a long line of old terraces.

We were all into stories of the area, but had never witnessed or experienced anything, so we boarded a train to the city on a cold winter's night not long prior to my leaving.

I really didn't know of their intentions until we arrived at the street of ill repute, and there laid out before us was a smorgasbord of semi-clad ladies of the night. There we wandered up and down to the cat-calls of the more experienced ladies wanting us to 'dip our wicks' sooner rather than later and calling us everything from pale little virgins to great lovers.

Soon after, we stopped to talk to a quite lady who seemed to be, as I recollect now, Northern Italian: we had grown up among varied nationalities then with my friends consisting of Polish, Italian,

Greek, Maltese and others. As a matter of fact, when I explained to my new buddies that my very first fumbling sexual encounter at thirteen was with a Maltese, they all laughed and said it was probably a Maltese Terrier.

This lady of the night was very friendly to us all, well-spoken and beautiful; I guessed her to be about twenty-five years old, slim and my height.

The boys then asked her:

"How much?"

"Ten dollars for straight up sex, that is all."

"Will you take seven as that's all we have and our friend is going away cause he's joined the navy?" said Les.

That was the first I heard of it, my introduction to getting laid that is.

"Ok," was all she said and with that I was literally pushed through the little gate into manhood.

Once inside I babbled on until she told me to relax and get undressed. Without thinking I stripped, much the same as when I had to undress for my physical in front of other boys, while men in uniform prodded us and felt our privates: cough, spread, spit, jump.

This time though, when I was down to nothing, she was very gentle and examined me thoroughly from head to toe while wiping my family jewels with a washer rinsed in diluted Dettol from a bowl beside the bed.

Then, without any fuss she took off her robe and lay down naked on the narrow bed. She was exquisite with her long dark hair, pale body, flat stomach and slightly trimmed pubic mound. Oh yes, we had seen photos of the Playboy girls and now this, the real thing.

She guided me all the way to a condom free climax like I never could have foreseen. And yes, no condoms were used at this time of our innocence and naivety.

Again, she washed me, then washed herself and we dressed in a comfortable silence. Before she opened the door to release me she emptied the bowl, washed it and then refilled it for her next client.

I felt a little betrayed, yet said goodbye to her as best I could under the circumstances.

My friends, old and new, loved my story and every word of it was true. She was truly divine, my first real lover, and it set an agenda for me in the future where I became somewhat fussy as to who would share my bed. Silly, hey? She was a prostitute after all. I'll tell you now though, she wasn't just any prostitute.

So the journey continued day after day. I had perched myself on a luggage rack and there I stayed reading and sleeping as often as possible until I earned the nickname 'crasher', and it stuck. I was always able to find a nook or cranny to sleep if I had to, and nothing would disturb me. It was my security blanket, my utopia, my womb to escape the turmoils of life, especially those I was about to face.

We picked up recruits in Melbourne and Adelaide then crossed the Nullarbor Plains, some three thousand miles of desert in the cold of winter, but we coped because we had our boy smells and confinement to keep us warm, although not too comfortable.

We met up with some serious lads along with some funny bastards, including Ron who was an ugly bugger and a *good hand* (a good bloke). He had smuggled on board a bottle of Bacardi and proceeded to get drunk mixing it with too little coke. His trick though was to drop his pants and light his farts, only this time with a belly full of rum, nylon underpants still attached to his bum and with legs up in the air he let go a ripper with a lighted match; the flame shot across the cabin and singed the boy opposite setting his comic alight. At the same time his undies caught fire and stuck to him while still burning, so amid the screams we doused him with cans of drink. The stench from burnt nylon, fart and flesh was so overwhelming within the confined space that two others who had been drinking began to vomit. We cleared out when the leading-seamen supervisors rushed in to see what all the fracas was about. First aid was administered and was to last the remainder of Ron's journey, then he was escorted to the sick bay on the base for treatment: he couldn't sit properly for weeks after.

He wasn't the only casualty to follow thanks to my being laid flat upon arrival at H.M.A.S. Leeuwin, our new home-to-be for the next year.

I had contracted the flu and didn't say anything to anyone immediately, which I should have since it would have saved me some grief.

We were issued with some basics and told to go to our living quarters to be assigned one of the four beds in each cubicle, known as *dongers*, given bedding and told to square up before the evening meal. Since we only had a few personal belongings, as instructed prior to us leaving our homes, we were to be *rekitted* the following day with new naval clothing and equipment.

My problem was shortly after I had made my bed and tidied up I collapsed and couldn't be woken even for a meal. Consequently I was left alone with my miserable flu. During these hours I overheard voices from what I could only describe as feral viciousness towards us new lads by our soon-to-be tormentors.

"We'll get this *new shit:*" as we became known in the months that followed, until the next intake arrived.

"Tonight, ok?" another voice.

"Yeah, lets fuck 'em right up."

With that they were gone, along with other mumblings I couldn't quite make out.

When the others returned I mentioned my misgivings to the division, comprising of about fifty lads. The other divisions would have to fend for themselves, since there wasn't any time to organise us, let alone them. Besides, I was too crook to concern myself as to their intentions, so I went back to bed.

Around midnight the shit hit the fan. We were jostled and pushed, punched and grabbed, our dongers turned upside down and some serious damage inflicted on those who resisted, including facial injuries, stitches and broken limbs when some were pushed down stairs and out of windows.

One poor bastard who had some personal hygiene problems was stripped naked and all his clothes and bedding thrown into the shower block where he was methodically scrubbed with a hard broom and washing powder. He looked as if he had been whipped after they had finished with him.

As for me, I was like a rag doll and too sick to care. No real physical damage because I had told my attackers I was fucking sick and didn't care what they did to me, or words to that effect.

My first encounter with reverse psychology seemed to work, to an extent.

The next day we presented ourselves to the sickbay and once they saw my dilapidated condition I was rushed off to the military hospital in Perth some forty miles from the base.

I was unconscious for about a week with double phenomena and nearly died. Then for another ten days I was ordered to recuperate while spitting sputum into a jar to see how the infection was clearing up.

When I returned things seemed to have settled down around the base with some form of normality and routine encompassing us, the new shit. I was left behind due to my absence and was assigned light duties for at least another fortnight; simultaneously having a profuse amount of dental work done by trainee hacks who eventually filled my teeth with so much metal that I was sure I could pick up the local radio station every time I opened my mouth. No bullshit: many suffered the same fate and in my case it would be years before this butchery could be rectified professionally.

To some extent the bullying had subsided, although I did hear a rumour of a case of buggery or two inflicted upon the defenceless. I'm at odds over this and I didn't actually witness any untoward sexual behaviour toward us boys, still there had been consenting intimate contact between a couple of queers. Again, so discreet I was never to observe such devious behaviour, *so perceived at the time.* Immediate dishonourable discharge from the service, with a recorded homosexual stamp over your record was the verdict and punishment imposed on those participating.

Boys playing boys games overzealously was acceptable, yet parents would have been shocked at their nature and intensity, I'm sure.

Not to throw dispersions upon our leader, a terrific able- seaman who nurtured us somewhat, who had separate accommodation beside our block, and always had pink towels and sheets hanging on his clothesline. We couldn't help but laugh and point fingers at them. After all, it was the first thing one saw when leaving our abode for morning parade.

As time went by and homesickness was the order of the day for most of us, I settled into a routine of extreme discipline, seamanship, shooting, all contact sports including boxing, gymnastics, bullying, bastardising and academic activities. We were boot-camp boys and it was survival of the fittest. Hadn't I joined to escape the controlling world of parents and a strict Catholic school where the cane or strap were used with free abandon?

Whether or not you were a pacifist it was all in for the boxing, gloves on, jump in and beat the shit out of each other. The winner to take on the next contender until there was only one boy standing.

Set up in weight divisions we fought on with black eyes, busted lips and an assortment of other injuries, all just to toughen us up, no doubt. I lasted about five bouts and was doing quite well, since my father had taught me a few tricks when fighting, until I ran into a junior 'Golden Gloves' out of Queensland who gave me a hiding for the first two rounds of our contest. I wanted to retire gracefully in the third but my corner kept me going until the end. I lost on points, just, thanks to gaining a new resolve with support from my division and winning the third; nevertheless I had had enough by this stage of the competition.

My best mate at the time, Jeff, was an all-round sportsman from the mountains, and a tough little bugger who befriended me before we had boarded the train to come to this brave new world. He was doing well in every bout until he took a blow to the back of the head and down he went; he never fully recovered. Although he achieved sportsman of the year when we graduated, he finally succumbed to his injuries soon after and was discharged medically unfit due to head trauma.

Next came target practice where we would hunker down into concrete trenches while holding up targets for the best and worst of the shooters who hit us with volley after volley of .303 full metal jackets. On one occasion I was holding my wooden handled target feeling the lead flay through the paper enemy and watching the bullets hit the dirt mounds a few metres behind our bunker, when my buddy sitting beside me was hit in the knee from a ricochet. The lead tore through his pants, chopping up his flesh somewhat with the bullet landing at my feet.

I yelled to the supervisor:

"John's been hit, let's get him the fuck out of here, and me along with him."

Without delay a halt was called and we all returned to the firing line while John went off to sickbay for some minor reattachment of his kneecap. Then it was my pleasure to shoot the crap out of everything I could see, but I couldn't hit the broad side of a ship I was that useless, especially with these antiquated First World War bolt action rifles. Eventually these antiques were replaced with the new Self Loading Rifle (SLRs) our soldiers were already using in action. I loved it when I switched over to automatic and blasted the hell out of the targets some two hundred yards away. The target operators, us included, had to withstand intense automatic fire after the delivery of these new weapons, so more protective clothing and helmets were at last issued. At times it felt as though the senior *top shits* wanted to fill us full of lead, such was the intensity of their fire. Or was it my imagination?

Our first shore leave after eight weeks of hell-on-earth, to the local township of Fremantle, was a nothing experience except more bitter homesickness while looking at the shops, invading the 'Flying Angle Club' for a pie and milkshake, and listening to the jukebox playing music that only made us more homesick.

These clubs, in almost every major capital city on the seaboard, were established to accommodate lonely sailors from naval ships stopping off in these ports. A home away from home you could say, yet some of these clubs I came to know had a notorious reputation, as I will explain later.

Some of the boys had sponsors who would come and take them into their homes, then return them to base on the Sunday afternoon. I wasn't in the least bit interested in putting up my hand to have these generous folk take me in, preferring to wallow in my own misery, boarding a train to Perth and sometimes beyond, heading back east, homeward bound.

I did gradually warm to the city and its friendly people, the parks, arcades, theatres and bakeries where I found one that served the most delicious strudel identical to how a school buddy's mum had made hers, a lifetime ago, in another world far, far away.

On one of these outings I had the pleasure of watching *The Sand Pebbles* at a theatre in the city and it instilled in me the original idea of wanting to be an engineer. Working alone in an engine room while having no regard for tradition or discipline inflicted upon me by an institution unable to connect with the very ranks that preserved the ship they depended on for their survival. A naïve arbitrary analysis I know; still, that's what I was about at the time. When Steve McQueen was called upon to perform above and beyond his call to duty he redeemed himself to the bitter end: his bitter end. I liked him; I liked his enigmatic coolness.

As time progressed we started to become more mischievous while on leave, with a group of us hanging around the local town on Saturday nights in our uniforms trying to attract the local girls. We only attracted the local hoods who would jump out of their cars with bats and an assortment of other not too lethal weapons, we had hoped. We would scatter like the little chickens we were, except for the few fearless fellow recruits who would take off after us when they saw the hopelessness of their plight.

One night we did wait in ambush with rocks and other missiles to launch at our transgressors, and when they stopped at a set of traffic lights we let them have it. At least forty missiles were launched simultaneously with most finding their target, breaking a couple of windows and depositing some nice dents in their precious bodywork.

We then scattered like wild young prey into the night. After all, we had become fit and could easily out sprint these fools.

This sweet revenge was reported to the base commander who reprimanded all on the base and stopped leave for a couple of weeks for every junior recruit.

These town cretins wanted charges laid by the local police, and payment for damages to the car. 'Fuck em,' we thought; so did the base commander who had considered these reprobates a thorn in his side for some time. After all, they had damaged his wards previously in various unprovoked assaults.

"Fuck em," was the catchcry for the week. Besides, as for cancelling our leave, we weren't eager to be seen on the streets after dark, not for some time anyway.

We had hell to pay from the seniors though when their leave was cancelled due to our misadventures. We were educated early by reason of, 'for every action there is an equal and opposite reaction' and the retribution to our persons by the recruits who had joined before us was definitive.

The grind continued for some months with most of us succumbing to the will of our masters. Discipline was swift and sure, although many of us tried to rebel, which only caused us more dilemmas.

Who am I kidding? We copped it from every angle whether defying the senior recruits and/or our captors. The institution had us by the balls and gave them a twist every minute of every day.

We retaliated any and every chance we were able, from smuggling grog onto the base by way of kindly older guys who would buy us our medicine-to-dull-the-senses, for a kickback of course, to the supply and distribution of adult magazines to satisfy the whims of the young man in all of us.

We had burrowed under perimeter fences and had to scatter on numerous occasions late some evenings when we were spotlighted smuggling our contraband into the base.

Some of us did the time, yet never gave up our suppliers and clients no matter what the punishment.

If our leaders couldn't bounce a coin off our tautly made bed then it was out to the parade ground with a rifle above your head for hours on end running in heavy boots, making it more difficult than it already was.

I had this privilege one winter morning in the rain when an earthquake hit us. The over-sized parade ground actually began to wave as if I was standing on a small boat with the wash of another larger boat hitting me. My punishment was suspended thanks to their concern for my welfare. The damage to the base and the old rifle I discarded was superficial. Running with a weapon was a moot point when I thought I was going to be sucked into the realms of another hell.

Other infringements to their law meant you could end up in the kitchen doing all and any dirty work they could find for you, including cleaning out the grease/sullage/slag traps. Have you cleaned out a heavily used sullage trap? Although this is a rhetorical question I can assure you it was easy to vomit while you were cleaning it, and that you would have to clean out too. It was fucking putrid, with all the malicious rotten fauna and flora you could possibly imagine floating there.

I was surprised the cooks took us under their wing though. This was to be the case throughout our junior years on other ships, especially those of us entering the engineering branch, before we had actually completed our marine technician course. There was always a deep-seated affinity between cooks and engineers going way back to who knows when. Could it be without food and thrust there wouldn't be a navy?

The cooks had some unconventional ideas thanks to their kitchen techniques, like boiling up a tray of lard and cracking a couple of dozen eggs into the little cups, then letting it set before closing up for the evening. They would hang them in the walk-in cool rooms, then in the morning would pop the trays into a preheated oven and, voila`: fried eggs for all, scooped from fresh boiling animal fat, thrown onto your plate along with lots of bacon on heavily buttered white toast, to be consumed by all with much a gusto.

Scran (shit cooked by the Royal Australian Navy) was always revered because we could be ourselves smoking duty free cigarettes and talking bullshit at the table. We had mastered the concept of attending scran later rather than be jostled out of the way by the top shit seniors who muscled their way in front of you. This practice caused some beatings outside the mess area for those who resisted this infringement to their rightful position on the food chain. Soon enough we all learned our place, after all, our time would come when we too became top shits.

One meal close to our hearts was corned beef and white sauce, which seemed to be the main evening fare every second night for the duration of my service. I still turn my nose up at it to this day, along with other copious repetitive provisions.

The cooks were always good sports, even when they yelled at you to get things done, but there was always a conversation and thanks, or pat on the back at the end of the day. They even laughed when they were told the food in the navy was terrific, until the cooks got to it: tucker fuckers.

The same could be said for myself years later when I had a small food establishment. I always made up for my aggression during busy periods by gathering all around me at the end of the evening, buying drinks and apologising for my bad behaviour, if necessary. I had always explained to my crew from the outset that the customers were our lifeblood and priority, so to get the job done was the core purpose of my/our little universe for those few intense hours.

✁✁✁✁✁✁✁✁✁✁✁✁✁✁✁✁✁✁✁

On our first leave for Christmas we were flown home in uniform much to the delight of our families waiting for us at the airport. We looked like kids from the navy cadets; still I had a good time anyway with a new girl, who was a family friend, waiting in the wings. For some reason my first real *squarie* (navy-speak for a serious girlfriend) had run off with someone else. I think it may have been due to the fact I was always depressed when I wrote or called; then who could blame her?

And so it was the first time I acquired 'lovers nuts' or 'blue balls', much to my mum's surprise and amusement, when the new girl and I were left alone in my room for some time. I didn't for the life of me know what was happening because I was in extreme testicular pain; as a result the girl left quickly, much to my embarrassment. My mother gave me a bag of frozen peas to ease the swelling, with nature taking its course later that night.

Also, it was my first encounter with aliens (or was I the alien within the new anti-establishment?) when I went to a school dance and was nearly punched out because I was wearing a uniform: my first encounter with the young anti-war movement. Luckily my old school buddies came to the rescue and after a minor scuffle we all got the hell out of there.

~~~~~~~~~~~~~~~~~~~

Summer 1969, we were close to becoming the top shit of the base, and yet we began to implode to an extent, with bullying rife among our own. If you weren't clean enough or your kit wasn't up to scratch you could be given the old scrubbing brush and hard broom treatment: very painful indeed.

Or the weaker were often set upon for being just that. Survival of the fittest, much the same as in William Golding's story, *Lord of the Flies*.

Unfortunately, those who couldn't keep up were sometimes the cause of punishment being metered out to others who were on the ball. Through no real fault of their own they were hounded and punished until some parents became involved and withdrew the boy(s) from the navy's clutches. No mean feat, since they had signed on for twelve years.

One such case was that of Arnold, an overweight fellow with the physique of a potato sack, flatfooted, legs that splayed out at the knees and a tongue that flicked out at you over a protruding lip when he spoke. He had no real academic ability either and was just so out of place in our rough and tumble world. His fellow inmates and instructors alike hounded the poor fellow day and night, and he was the cause of more punishment being metered out to others due to his inability to perform in the gym, on the parade ground, keeping his area tidy, his bed made to order, boots shining, et cetera: you name it, he couldn't do it correctly.

I could never figure out why recruits like Arnold where inducted in the first place. Did they think they could make a man of him, or was it just a sadistic streak running through the system at the time, knowing full well these unfortunate sorry lads were to be the centre of all our frustrations, us and instructors alike?

Many years later I was to hear that Arnold sued the navy for psychological damage arising during his year in basic training, and won.

I was involved in an incident were I had to beat up a fellow recruit or be beaten myself by other bullies in the dormitory. I did this despicable act with a conscience and then disassociated myself from these idiots who I thought were my friends.

I later spoke to my victim and apologised for my actions.

He said to me:

"Bru, I forgive you, and I know what would have happened to you if you didn't fight me, so I didn't fight back because I wanted it to be over quickly, and now I'm going home."

"What, why?" I was taken aback. "What's happened?"

"Mom and dad are coming over to take me home and I'm going back to school."

I was gutted, ashamed. You name it, I was it. And I never really had the stomach for fighting from then on. I didn't partake upon a rampage of violence and destruction on the new shits when they finally arrived either.

I hope he went on to bigger and better things. I know I didn't for many, many years.

Also, my cousin, Gary, joined six months later even though I tried to warn him this was no picnic. I did endeavour to be the good top shit so his stay there wouldn't be too difficult.

Did I do a good enough job? I don't know to this day because, I feel, he has become a bit of a loner insofar as reconnecting with his navy buddies, and works for himself in his one-man business well away from the clutches of anything navy.

All was not doom and gloom though with an amusing incident I recall when we discovered amongst us a real 'wanker'. He would be at it any and every chance he could, but was never harassed owing to his likeable personality, in that he was a constant source of amusement to us all. One night he was taking a late shower, so we thought we would surprise him and give him a hard time. When we walked around the corner he was at it again, in the shower cubicle, and when we began giving him hell all he said was:

"It's my cock and it's my soap, I'll wash it as fast as I like."

We all fell about laughing, then left him to his own devises.

Talking about that part of the anatomy: at our farewell dinner dance just prior to our graduation we were all dressed in pristine uniforms, the shine on our shoes like mirrors to our souls, and with a new found set of balls we conducted ourselves as we should in front of our leaders, officers, guests and the base commander alike, along with all their wives and partners, daughters and their female friends from across the small city of Fremantle attending the recruits' passing-out ball.

Cameras flashed, dancing, live music, no alcohol for us top shits, bantering, nudging and generally a frivolous time was had by us all. Until Andy, a funny bastard if ever there was one, put tiny mirrors on the tips of his boots allowing him to see up the dresses of the girls. He was sprung by one of his victims, slapped senseless and had to flee outside prior to his identity being disclosed to senior personnel.

We were aware of his identity and while laughing to ourselves we said to our leaders we couldn't pinpoint the cad.

As the night wore on one of the better looking guys told me he had gotten a hand job from one of the girls, and then pointed her out to me. We had managed to smuggle a small quantity of spirits into the function and mixed it with a soft drink or two, thus giving me just enough courage to approach this girl and ask her to dance. After all, I wasn't one of the tall, dark and handsome crew who could just snap a finger to attract a lady.

On the dance floor she made a comment of how cute I was and I reciprocated with a ditto type remark. 'Cute. Piss off', I thought, then I asked her if she wanted to go outside for some fresh air. Being winter it was cold out but otherwise not too bad, so with nothing to lose I came straight out with it and said:

"Would you give me a hand-job?"

"If you want," was all she said.

We then went around the side of the gymnasium where the dance was being held and stood against the wall. She then unzipped my trousers and wrapped her cold, yet warm hand around my boyhood, pulled it out and proceeded to expertly stroke it. I've got to say she was doing a better job than I could have done at the time, and with her expertise I came too quickly (so she said). With well-aimed precision I even managed to hit the toe of her shoe, but didn't say anything because she had walked over to the grass to wipe her hand. I could only describe it as the most exciting hand-job I had ever wet-dreamed of prior to her intervention, then and there outside the hall of horrors that had previously caused us so much pain during our tenure.

All she said to me before she went inside was:

"See ya." And sadly my love affair within the confines of H.M.A.S. Leeuwin was over.

Of course I bragged the next day to all who would listen, until I was informed she might have been one of our arch pain-in-the-arse nemesis' daughters. A mean spirited superior we came to dislike intensely over our time and whose wife, we joked, was probably giving hand-jobs, or worse, to other sailors, along with his daughter.

~~~~~~~~~~~~~~~~~~~~

"Bruhwiller, get that bloody breathing apparatus on and get into that container. We're going to fill it with smoke and you'll have to find your way out in pitch darkness," said our instructor. These instructors usually had the official rank of a 'leading or able seaman', the equivalent of a corporal or a private in the army. They were to be called *sir* until you were out of the training institution, and their clutches.

Not only was there one huge steel container, but four, joined end to end with hatchways separating each of these metal boxes, much the same as shipping containers. This was a simulated exercise for a bombed or torpedoed ship and your reaction to surviving by crawling through a labyrinth of compartments in darkness and smoke to escape, and survive.

"Like fuck you say." We were top shits by now and these last training exercises, just a few weeks before our departure and our farewell dance, were becoming more elaborate and dangerous.

"What was that Bruhwiller?"

"Nothing sir." It gave me the shits all through my time served that my surname always put me on the top rungs of any situation where alphabetical order was initiated. I was becoming cheeky too and answered back on numerous occasions, getting me into all sorts of trouble.

"Just get the fuckin' thing on and get in there," he said.

"Are you coming in to save us if it all goes to shit?" I said out loud.

"Don't fuckin' worry about it. Move!" said the now pissed-off instructor.

We were all worried about it though, with many panicking and having to be pulled out. I was ok, this time, although as new lads we were put through the 'survival at sea' exercise, which can only be described as harrowing. Being thrown into water fully clothed and told to tread water for half hour then swim two hundred metres, tread water again, until you drowned, or nearly drowned, as was my tenebrous experience. It put the fear of Christ into me for sure, and I wasn't the only one who came out feeling a little reticent about the dangers of water.

Finally, just prior to our departure from Van Diemen's Land, we had to individually front a small board of officers comprising of specialists in their chosen fields, some with university degrees, to determine what branch of the service you would be best suited.

No matter what you thought you would like to do, they invariably had the notion of you being slotted into areas where you were most needed.

I had some decent advise from a senior some months before (not all were bullies) to stand up and demand your career of choice, and if you presented a solid case then the chances of you securing your chosen field would be realised. I did just that and was allowed to enter the diesel engineering branch. I thought, 'Small ships just like Steve McQueen on the Sand Pebbles', and maybe submarines. I was still sixteen years old.

Yes, 1968 changed me, and by mid-1969 I was unrecognisable, especially to myself.

2nd Chapter

THE VUNG TAU FERRY
(My rusty nail)

'Life is an abnormal business.'
Eugene Ionesco
(The Rhinoceros)

I joined the H.M.A.S. Sydney at Cockatoo Island before my seventeenth birthday in mid-1969 while it was being rejuvenated for another trip to Vietnam.

The ship was a mess with dockyard workers everywhere and as a result we were left to our own devises, to an extent. That is, apart from menial tasks like cleaning, painting, mess/kitchen duties there was no real running-a-ship routine owing to very few officers being on board supervising. Of course we had the customary chiefs and non-commission seniors to direct us, otherwise we would scamper off on the workboat to Garden Island, down the hill from Kings Cross, to drink, gamble and chase women, preferably ones we didn't have to pay for.

It was a free-for-all with the Yanks in town on *R and R* from the war zone, with plenty of money, drugs, gambling and ladies-of-the-night to go around.

The place was a mad house, nevertheless we settled into a routine spending time with all types of permissive and debauched individuals of the night. Gay and lesbian haunts, strip palaces, bars, clubs and late night venues; here we would eventually meet the underside of life including strippers, crooks, whores and the Les Girls entourage. It was at this particular time that the mafia was making their churlish attempt to infiltrate our club scene, much to the displeasure of some local guard: Abe Saffron excluded.

All good clean fun as far as we were concerned, although some members of our young troupe did eventually fall into the dark circle of life.

In my description of our time here at the Cross I will not castigate and disclose the identities of any individuals and their follies, but my own deeds will be laid bare for all to judge and why not? That's why I'm here writing my story. Anyway, it was just our time, and with the speed of the apocalyptic nature of things that kept spinning around us, we all considered our time was coming, as did many others inside and outside of the armed forces. The world was being tipped onto its ear, so we were going to make the most of it.

While we're here in this part of my tome I will encapsulate the time I served in and around this den of iniquity into the present chapter, since some of the incidents juxtaposed themselves over a period of time.

We were forbidden to wear our uniforms ashore, yet there were plenty of uniforms in the Cross. We surmised the anti-war cretins at the time weren't fearless enough to enter this forbidden city, and so it was, uniforms or no, the area was a go-zone for us all. Venturing outside our world may have seen a different outcome thanks to servicemen in uniform being assaulted and spat on by the insipid individuals waving their peace banners in wild abandon.

I really couldn't see the point of Vietnam myself at the time, likewise with many of my comrades serving; we just did as we were told to hold it all together. We believed, like the peace-loving and harmless hippies, that 'fighting for peace was like fucking for virginity' (anti-war graffiti), but it was those other individuals who did actually condemn, ridicule and spit on us who should now hang their heads.

These transgressors would not have survived under any other governments' other than their own open democracies, *their* western governments, the very democracies they were fighting against.

~~~~~~~~~~~~~~~~~~~~

We were sitting at the far end of a bar in the Venus Room, this being a crime den if ever there was one, full of the types you wouldn't bring home to mother, when a shot rang out, then two more in quick succession scattering hoods, standover men, hookers, Yanks in uniform and an assortment of other individuals who usually felt right at home there.

The manager of the bar, also a standover man himself, had shot and killed another standover crook, known as The Glove, so named because he wore a lead lined glove to beat his victims to a pulp. He pleaded self-defence and was freed without conviction, such was the corruption within the senior echelons of the state government and the police command at the time. He had shot The Glove in the back.

We jumped and ran, only to find out all the details soon after. Big Jim Anderson was the shooter and right-hand man for Abe Saffron who also owned The Carousel and Les Girls, all of which we frequented, along with thousands of others, I'm sure. Anderson also ran a brothel above the Venus Room and was a mate of Lennie McPherson who was a force to be reckoned with if you ever crossed him. However, we were left alone along with all those who were innocent and willing to spend their money. After all, we were their lifeblood. Funny thing though, there never seemed to be any real trouble among the punters; then again, retribution from these hard men would be swift and sure if you did cross them.

They liked us youngsters, especially if we wore our uniforms, which we did on occasion in defiance of the directive issued us at the time, due to our spending ability and the fact we were servicemen, much the same as their fathers were, I surmised. After all, the country was built on the lives of our forefathers, the blood spilt overseas and now here as well, in the underworld. I guess they considered that was what *their* democracy was all about, albeit a corrupt one, as was the case then. This world had indeed become a continuing test of survival.

Big Jim eventually grassed on Abe, which saw his downfall by way of the Crime Commission after Saffron locked him out of his underworld. Jim had all the guff because he handled the black books for Abe.

The girls would bid us welcome everywhere we ventured within the confines of this gun-toting territory and we even had the pleasure of meeting a few of the Kings of the Cross including Mr McPherson, who incidentally, I happened to rent premises from some years later. Actually, the property belonged to his sister and I think she introduced him to me as a warning not to dud her in any way. I couldn't and wouldn't have.

Now, let me say, dope was pushed onto us so we could sell it to our shipmates, which we declined gracefully, although some did take them up on their offer only to find themselves in a world of hurt if they didn't get back to the owners of the said products with the correct gratuity.

Many poor bastards in the navy would spend their pay the first night out on gambling, prostitutes and drugs, then live on board their respective ships or bases until the following fortnightly payday.

Some had sunk themselves into all sorts of trouble if they cared to venture out without cash in their pockets, getting themselves drunk on visitors' generosity and then being accosted and brutalised in more ways than one. Some even went to the extent of prostituting themselves out to a local degenerate who happened to be a senior law council: he would drive around the area and offer you ten bucks if you would let him suck your cock. This fellow was also associated with a group of fellow depraved lunatics who would offer big bucks if you would go to a flat nearby and actually defecate onto a glass table with them peering at you from underneath. Many did for a quick buck, and no, I didn't.

The Americans would buy us drinks all night because they liked us and had months of pay to deplete while on leave; even so far as shouting us the occasional good time girl. At times we would end up at Les Girls upstairs after their show and the ensemble themselves, being a good bunch of guys/gays, never interfered with us except on an invitation from the odd guest among us.

These men in drag were somewhat more attractive than the girls on the street or in the brothels, to a degree. An acquaintance who had had a similar fling with a boy/girl on Singapore's Boogie (Bugis) Street told us he was so drunk every night while on leave there, that he was unaware he was banging a boy until the last night because, he explained, he wasn't as drunk as he had been the previous two nights. Such was the resolve of these Asian boys to present themselves as women. He said now he could always tell though, due to the fact the boys in drag were more attractive than the women. I guess he had a taste for them after that, considering he once said to me in a singsong voice:

"Women are ok, but there's nothing like the real thing."

And why, you may ask, did we frequent clubs like Les Girls? Simply because it attracted girls, who are so aptly described these days as fag hags, and other attractive curious ladies who were beginning to find their own feet in a modern world.

In the nineties the Wood Royal Commission found corruption went to the highest ranks of the powerful within the police force and the state government, including also, a small element in the federal police. Yet the police in general metered out their own form of justice; moreover, it was safe to walk the streets within the ordinary community, unlike today. Condone or condemn, ninety per cent, whether on the take of not, did their job. And communities away from these crime jungles felt they could leave their doors unlocked if they chose in those early days a couple of generations ago. They were all bloody hard men.

~~~~~~~~~~~~~~~~~~~

Back on board my ship, just prior to leaving for the war zone, there was still major work to be done with the resupplying of stores to cater for a thousand plus personnel, painting and cleaning after the repairs, refuelling from scratch with ship and aviation fuels for us, the army contingent, and all their supplies for fighting a war.

We carried bulk food, beer, ammunition, machine lubricants and parts: you name it we carried it up ramps and down into the holds (oh! the haemorrhoids). We were thrown into dark pits to recoat fuel and water tanks much to the disgust of all those involved, including myself. Supplied with breathing apparatus we still had to be dragged out after fifteen minutes, conscious or unconscious, to be relieved by others.

We re-lagged superheated steam pipes with buckets of moistened asbestos that hardened (much the same as plaster setting on a broken limb) to form a heatproof protective cover. These pipes could become so hot that if a flange or join split and you were unlucky enough to be in close proximity, or standing below the offending pipe, it could cut you in half as easily a hot knife through butter.

We chipped away at old paint with Jason pistols, which were a type of hand jackhammer with a bunch of nail-like contacts coated with beryllium used to prevent sparking. As I have previously explained, this toxic substance if inhaled for any length of time will cause simular lung diseases to asbestos and the odd spark could have been catastrophic with all the munitions and fuels on board.

Eventually we soon had become disillusioned with working and living in a metal box, and as a result I took off for a non-approved vacation on my newly purchased motorcycle: a Suzuki as I recall. From there it all went downhill with it culminating in me having to spend some time in the *brig*.

Initially a few of us went A.W.O.L, that is, absent without leave, or 'Ackwillie' as some of the old timers referred to it, including my grandfather who was a veteran of both World Wars.

We holiday makers had split up only to find ourselves caught by the Naval Police after a few days and thrown into *slots* (slots and brig are naval detention centres), where we shared cells with lots of American boys who were determined not to return to Vietnam under any circumstances, even to the extent of self- harm. One of which succeeded in ending it himself just before we were to be processed for incarceration. His partly covered body, now blue from self-strangulation and rigor mortis, was carried from his cell on a stretcher as we waited in a separate area for processing.

Our fellow inmates showed us some of the most horrific photos I have ever seen of the carnage from both sides including bodies blown to bits, burnt from napalm, shot, headless or beheaded with limbs hacked as well. You name it I saw it through their own lenses, and through the hollow eyes that now guided them through what remained of their lives.

Talk about 'winning the hearts and minds' of the locals from a different perspective other than that of the allied forces in a foreign land. The Viet Cong had it down to a fine art by raping and killing the youngest daughter of a village leader in front of all in the village, including the father himself, or lopping off the newly inoculated arms of children, and maybe a leg or two. These inhuman acts kept their own ambitions alive in winning their war by putting the fear of Buddha, or any other deity in which they believed, into the villagers. That was their answer to winning the locals' hearts and minds. It worked, didn't it?

My incarceration lasted a couple of weeks before I was returned to my ship and in that time my eyes were well and truly opened to the horrors of life in and out of a combat zone. Some there had written letters proclaiming their support for Che Guevara and the new revolution, which was all the rage then, so they would be discharged unsuitable and a communist. It didn't work because it was seen to be a tactic to get oneself out of the clutches of their tormentors.

I had become antagonistic to my captors stemming from arduous conditions, lack of freedom, servitude to the many bosses I had, the bullying and the general sore arse from being kicked around from pillar to post by the too many Chiefs and not enough Indians syndrome. Later I identified this with The Stockholm Experiment, where men in control of other men become belligerent and vindictive toward their charges.

A little later I went to visit old school friends, on an official leave pass this time, for a couple of weeks prior to sailing for waters unknown, and thought I might reacquaint myself with a couple of girls from my schooldays, get drunk, wildly push my bike to its limits and return to Kings Cross to again discover the delights of my first real sexual encounter with my lady-of-the-night. I had, on a couple of previous occasions, made a half-hearted attempt to find her, but to no avail. As I became a little more acquainted with this class of woman I realised she may have just been passing through, such was her beauty and quiet demeanour compared to the others.

To date I had dodged my parents who were annoyed with me for skipping out previously without leave, but generally I was going to have a fine old time breaking from society and naval restraints.

I was at a navy mate's party one Saturday in the mountains and had drunk myself into a melancholy state, aching for the innocence of my lost youth, and as a result I decided to leave around nine that evening to go and see my folks, then return to my ship.

I took a bend a little too fast half way down the mountain road towards the city, skidded on gravel, hit a guidepost and tumbled down an embankment; the bike took off in another direction to God knows where.

I crawled my way back to the road and lay there for, I think, about fifteen minutes before a car stopped to investigate this body lying on the side of the road. From there an ambulance was called to take me back up to the local hospital in the mountains where I was diagnosed with concussion, multiple cuts and abrasions, with some heavy bruising and a knee injury.

No breaks according to the x-rays, however, a hospital stay was inevitable. I said to the nurses not to contact my parents and that I would call them the next day so as not to worry them in the middle of the night.

The following day they were up at the hospital like a shot from a .303, and shortly after were back again to collect me and take me home for a few days R and R before returning me to my ship. All ok by me, although my stay at home was to be a little longer than first expected.

Comfortable in my old bed, or on the lounge at home, I felt my early youth returning and this made me feel both heartened and lost simultaneously. Why, oh why, had I insisted on leaving my home, family and friends to set out on an adventure I wasn't ready for?

Then out of the blue my parents received a phone call from the police saying they had some disturbing news as to my whereabouts and they had a search party looking for my body at the base of a cliff up in the mountains.

"Yes," my dad said, "You say you're looking for my son's body? Where, how.....I don't understand."

Mum came rushing, thinking, panicking after dad called out and dropped the phone. It could only be my brother Michael, but he was in Vietnam. I calmed immediately thinking it was some mistake when my mother took control of the situation.

"He's here, with us," mum said. "Hikers found a motor bike at the base of a cliff," she repeated. "And you have confirmed it belonged and is registered to Mark," she repeated again.

"No, he's here, now, and recovering after a hospital stay up there."

"I have no idea how he managed to survive and climb up a ninety foot cliff," said mom, answering the policeman's question.

"Well, thank you. It's all ok. Sorry to have put you through all that trouble....the search party and all. Yes, I'll tell him to call you when he's up and about." She hung up then.

"What the bloody hell was that all about?" said my father.

"I know I didn't climb any cliff to get to the road and that's for sure," I said. "I must have been on a ledge or something."

With that they took me off to church the following day.

The bike was irreparable, obviously, and the damage to my helmet was extensive with a hole through the front and out the side approximately where my eye may have been, had it not been for my crash hat.

Later when we actually saw the wreck I could see where the rear view mirror had snapped off and the metal spike remaining on the handlebars had been the cause of the helmet damage. And to think I only wore head protection because it had been cold that night. My guardian again at work: I certainly had kept him/her busy to date.

Just prior to our departure for Vietnam our leaders decided it would be a good idea if we newcomers have a very real fire drill off the ship, but still in the dockyard were the work had been carried out during the overhaul.

They set fires up at the mouth of old shipping containers, much the same as our survival at sea exercise a few months previously, where smoke was pumped into simular containers and we had to grope our way out.

After having been given all the instructions necessary I was again alphabetically called upon to extinguish the bloody thing.

Hazard reduction clothes on, high pressure hose in hand… whoosh! I hit it too low and was immediately engulfed in flames for what seemed to be too long. I was pulled out of the hot zone and taken to the nearest medical facility with what may have been serious burns. I had no major injuries; nevertheless, I had no hair on my arms, face/eyebrows, and legs. The fire wasn't supposed to have been too large, yet it had gotten out of control somewhat, as fires do, and the gear I had been provided was not adequate enough to protect me from the intensity of this particular exercise. I wore a reddish pink tinge over hairless pale white skin for ages; a leper wouldn't have laid me, such was my grotesque appearance.

~~~~~~~~~~~~~~~~~~~

We left Sydney Harbour in the early morning under a security blanket, such was the routine in war time with a full complement of troops and sailors, but not before my parents were asked to sign a release for their son to enter a war zone due to my being underage.

Of course I had pressured them to sign, because in the eyes of my shipmates and superiors I didn't want to be seen as a child tied to mum's apron strings. I would say other youngsters in my position did much the same to go on this voyage, along with some twelve hundred plus able bodies who didn't need a chit to die, if necessary. Our ship was also loaded with munitions and weapons, light spotter aircraft, helicopters, armoured vehicles, jeeps, landing craft and an assortment of other potential death-causing equipment.

Secrecy was the order of the day for this converted aircraft carrier, since it could have been a target for any would-be enemy, including the self-sacrificing terrorist who, for the advancement of their communist take-over in their beleaguered country, would blow themselves and others to kingdom come.

Nothing changes, does it? There will always be the bloody-minded bastards willing to kill themselves and others for their greater good/god: innocent women and children included.

The Vung Tau Ferry was a small British carrier christened the H.M.S. Terrible when first launched in 1944, which we had purchased from them after World War Two to replace the H.M.A.S. Sydney sunk by the Germans in 1941. It served with distinction in the Korean campaign until 1952 and remained in commission until 1958, then recommissioned as a troop transport in 1962. We had prolonged its life with paint and spit for the job it had been doing for a few years before it became my home.

It was maintenance personified day and night to keep it afloat and functioning; still we grew to respect this ship for its tenacity and resolve to keep going.

We were now referred to as 'ordinary seamen' or *pussers* (although all sailors were known as pussers), a rank below that of an 'able seamen' and a rank above a 'junior recruit'. We were to hang onto this lowly position for the time we served on this ship, being at least six months, and in some cases a full year, then it was off to training in our respective fields before gaining the rank of able seaman.

You can imagine the jobs we were ordered to carry out, day and night, fair wind or foul, such as cleaning the *heads* (toilets) and showers; not with our toothbrushes, akin to the order if we misbehaved or showed signs of uncleanliness back in recruit school. Mopping, cleaning, kitchen slaves, laundry, engine room labourers and painting over more rust than you could ever chip off. Now multiply most of this work by three due the compliment of *pongos* (army personnel) we were transporting to Vietnam, and also returning with some of the poor lads who preferred not to fly home after suffering a year there.

We just kept our mouths shut and did as we were told otherwise a sore arse was in the offing. Not wanting to volunteer for any vile work was as much a part of the trip as just getting through it with the least amount of grief, that is, keeping a low profile throughout the journey. If you were to put your hand up you then became a recognisable target for future deplorable work deployment.

Our sleeping arrangements were, due to a lack of room, primitive, as were the army boys' bed allocations. Bedding was just thrown anywhere you could find a spare piece of deck and it was first in best dressed for all concerned. While we were separated from the pongos we all shared the facilities when the situation arose. Timing of showers and toilets was critical, yet if we were on late *watches, such as the evening of first watch, it was pure bliss because when the army was bedded down we could then have some quiet time to ourselves. I grew to love the late shifts whether in the engine room, laundry and even the kitchen after dinner or before breakfast when there was no pressure to perform your duties, nevertheless you would perform all the duties allocated you adequately otherwise trouble would befall you from a great height.

I had managed to grab a cushioned bench seat not two feet wide that semi-surrounded the sleeping areas, and there I laid my hammock, and there it stayed for the whole trip along with my kit, which consisted of navy issued uniforms, work clothes and accessories stored there also, and nothing was going to move me. Some actually secured their hammock to points on the bulkhead, but they were the diehard fans of the swinging dick mentality.

Always wanting to be on top of you and when they fell out there was hell to pay and damage done to those sleeping on the deck below them. Securing a piece of bench space in a corner saved me no end of grief and 'the crasher' was left amicably to his own devises for most of the trip.

We had been at sea for only a few days when:

"Bruhwiller, you do the heads this morning and it's your job for your eight hours on, ok?"

"Sir."

"I'm a chief petty officer, so call me chief, ok?"

"Chief."

"You know where the stores are so get your arse down there and grab mops and buckets and plenty of disinfectant, ok?"

"Ok."

I had heard rumours that the pongos' quarters were a mess, thanks to their lack of seamanship and wobbly sea legs, yet our time already served had allowed us to attain most sea-going abilities, only to a certain extent though.

I carried all the cleaning gear I could so I wouldn't have to climb back into the hold to grab extra supplies because I wanted to finish the chore as quickly as possible.

"Fuck me," I said to myself when I saw the state of the heads the pongos had defiled, although what hit me first was the smell, or should I say, the vengeful presence of some foreign hell I could never have imagined, and I had been into some putrid places in the line of duty so far.

"Fucking hell, how in the fuck am I supposed to clean up this shit hole?" I said out loud.

With that an officer strode past, stopped, looked, sniffed then without a sideways glance, said:

"Good luck, sailor," and walked off.

There was vomit; there was shit; there were cigarettes butts; there was piss and copious amounts of loo paper, and it was all sloshing around my boots up to my heels. The cubicles.....well, the cubicles I won't go into, and didn't.

So it began with rubber gloves, rain boots that I had commandeered after protesting to the chief, and a hose not normally used for cleaning toilets and showers. I then began the task at hand.

The showers were not much different; not as bad, so after I vomited I commenced on them.

I had the pleasure of this duty on a number of occasions, although none as putrid as the first. Things and stomachs seemed to settle down somewhat as we sailed further into the fog of our lives, away from the security of our homes.

"Bullwinkle, engine room, mid watch." A new nickname!

'Beauty,' I thought. Even though it was bloody hot down there it was the cool of the early morning, on top of a feed of bacon and eggs grilled on the flange of a super-heated steam pipe at four a.m. that was the pay-off. When the cooks were stumbling into the *galley* (kitchen) we ambushed them for the best officers *vittles* ('God made the vittles, but the devil made the cook'- quote/anon) and after devouring our rations I would shower before the shit hit the fan with the morning wake up calls. This middle watch seemed to make it all worthwhile for me.

It still doesn't worry me the flange cover was an asbestos cap easily lifted off and replaced, it was still the best serve of tucker on the whole voyage.

Who recognised the dangers of working with asbestos then? It was just a mix and lag protection for superheated steam pipes.

Other meals were a nightmare for all concerned, including the cooks and us ordinary seamen, who toiled day and night to feed all the hungry mouths on board, until eventually we depleted the stores to such an extent that Chico rolls and corned beef with white sauce was the main diet for most, along with powdered eggs, powdered potato and powdered milk with breakfast cereal or porridge. The coffee was woeful according to all and sundry; the tea was just that.

However, when it came time to knock off for the day and we weren't rostered on an overnight watch, we would all grab our twenty-six ounce (750ml) tin of Reches beer rations and watch a movie in the hanger smoking our cheap duty-free smokes. Come to think of it, even if you were rostered on a late night shift you would still grab your beer ration even though it was forbidden to drink immediately prior to a watch.

This issuing of beer rations is where our black market became a reality. If the pongos, or our own crew, didn't want their ration we would pay them to get in line and get their beer for us, then using our new found engineering skills we would reseal the cans using all and any means to keep the beer alive and fresh, depending on the size of the holes punched into the top of the cans: no ring-pulls back then.

We would have to befriend and pay off these can-destroyers occasionally, so as to keep the holes to the smallest possible circumference due to the contraption they used in front of the officer-of-the-watch on duty at the time. They would be ordered to punch a small hole in one side of the can lid while at the same time the device would put a larger hole on the other side.

With the system manipulated we would easily drink four cans quickly before they went flat and warm, simultaneously selling the other beers at exorbitant prices to the less fortunate participants while watching movies.

We always had access to the kitchen, since we spent so much time there working, and again, the cooks looked after us. It must have been due to our prowess in cleaning up their mess on a daily basis. With their blessing we even managed to store beer in the cold rooms if the cans were properly resealed. Of course a gratuity had to be paid.

I continually volunteered for working below decks in the engine room doing evening watches because I liked the noise and the solitude to a certain extent. Apart from what was generally called *punching sprayers* for any extended period it was an easy taskmaster. The power plant consisted of four three-drum boilers sending muscle via steam turbines to the twin propellers, and consistently changing leak-proof copper fuel washers while they were firing was what we called punching sprayers; it was bloody hot work while munching on salt tablets. There were many dangers in the engine room, let me assure you, from tumbling down ladders due to oily boots, steam burns to heat exhaustion; head knocks to broken bones, and hearing problems from the continuous noise. And let's be frank here, wearing earmuffs was not obligatory when you couldn't hear anyone or anything with them on by way of warnings and instructions. They were uncomfortable and hot in this environment to boot.

I guess my time overall on this voyage was one of injury unfortunately, with a tumble injuring my hip, minor burns, abrasions and heat stroke, yet all in all it gave me a form of anonymity down amongst the noise and the heat, for which I was grateful. Some injuries I witnessed though were not minor especially when a steam pipe would burst and burn an unsuspecting rating standing in the wrong place at the wrong time.

Times in between work could be refreshing especially when it came to listening to the dulcet tunes of the army and navy bands playing their repertoire in between firing practice, cat-calls, yelling and groans of the troops ready to enter a war zone, along with fighting us navy boys in the ring.

Thanks to the fact their frustrations and ours were many and varied we punched the hell out of each other in an organised tournament to vent our spleens. In this controlled circumstance I was encouraged to have a go owing to previously fighting to an acceptable standard while in recruit school. How long did I last? Not long, and some even lost money on me, but what the heck, they were stupid to bet for a team that had less to lose than the pongos going to war. Their fight was within themselves, their fear was their power and in their minds their punch was a life-saving punch, since they were soon to be in the fight of their lives. This boxing was just a practice run.

Other frustration relieving exercises without damaging each other was volleyball and the like, but the most enjoyable of all, for me anyway, was the expenditure of weaponry ammunition into an otherwise harmless ocean.

"Get all the ammo and weapons you can carry from the store room Bruhwiller and get it up to the flight deck asap."

"What's going on chief?"

"We're going to blast the shit out of everything we can possibly throw over the side, including you, so get moving." He was happy though, as was I.

"Get the SLRs, 45s (big bore hand guns) and you'll need extra hands for the 50 cal heavy machine guns and any other automatic weapons you can find, ok?" said the chief. "And ask the duty officer for the keys and he will see you right with extra bodies to help you. We're going to see who shoots the best, us or the pongos."

With that I was off like a scorched rabbit to do the best I could by destroying all sea life under withering fire.

Now don't be too critical, such was the safety factor to all this insofar as disbursing potentially dangerous munitions before it corroded, as did everything from salt percolation.

Also, it gave us all practice on how better to kill those who may have the inkling to kill us. Besides, it helped to ease the army's boredom.

Balloons, empty drums and containers, both large and small, from as far and wide as the kitchen, engine room and store rooms supplied us with our targets, while us lucky ones had our time behind the weapons of destruction.

It was like something out of those gangster movies where the hoods stand together blasting away at their opposition. It concerns me now how all that lead has affected the environment over the years, not just from us, but also from all the carnage on the high seas. Still, back then it was pure fun and one of the highlights as we fought for control of points and damage done to the unfortunate floating objects. Who won? No one cared.

I had just finished touch-up painting and carving my initials into the Bofors on the starboard side of the ship when a gunnery officer informed me they wanted to use this 40mm cannon to let off a few rounds, and steam no doubt. An automatic firing anti-aircraft smallish cannon, one of four positioned on both sides of the ship, were a deterrent while seagoing in the war zone, on the *gunline*; this ammunition needed to be expended also, for the same reasons as previously mentioned.

"Sir," I said. "Could I have a go at it please sir?"

"Do you want to be a gunner after you leave here?"

"Yes sir," I lied.

So, after some instruction from the experienced I was seated on the stool, positioned my sights and away I went pumping a half dozen shells into the unknown. I took my eyes away from the sights and whoomp, whoomp, whoomp as they sank a far off nothing. It was pure bliss.

Years later I was visiting the war museum in our nation's capital, when lo and behold, there was a bofors from my ship sitting there for all to see. And to this day if you look carefully, really carefully, there, well painted over, are the initials MB.

One evening, not too far from our destination, we were all ordered to attend a film experience in the lower hanger. What was this? A warry or some such exciting visual treat.

The place was abuzz when the lights went out and a voice from a pulpit announced we were about to see perverse images and film regarding sexual transmitted diseases, so as to prepare us all for Asia's ladies of the night, and day. We all immediately pricked up our ears, lit our smokes, gulped our beers and for once an officer had our undivided attention.

I've never seen so much genital hardware in so bad a repair as these, and the fact we were told some of these poor bastards who owned these festered remnants of manhood would never be allowed to return home due to their wayward behaviour, and were to be kept in an institution somewhere to die the miserable death of a pox ridden leper.

Penises and testicles dangling off near rotten torsos infected with puss filled tennis ball sized lesions all enough to make grown men vomit. Women's privates were unfurled too; not at all pleasant, although not as visually disturbing, yet just enough damage to be on the lookout when diving, and then to back away from if one was sober enough or could see in the dark.

The medical officer castigated our innocence and our self-gratifying sixties free love attitudes even though some there were still virgins.

He said to us:

"Wear those fucking rubbers you numbskulls, or die, and take the bloody thing off as soon as you have shot your load."

He went on:

"If you're pissed and leave it in there to soak you *will* catch the pox, do you all understand?"

"Do you all understand me, I can't hear you?" He bawled.

"Yes sir."

"And another thing, if you're stupid enough to stick your dick into something without a condom here's what I recommend you do. Are you listening?"

"Yes sir."

"Pull your thing out of whatever you have penetrated and piss into your cupped hands, then wash all you private parts with your own urine. This clears your tubes and disinfects the surrounding area."

We all gasped at the thought then realised the benefits of a longer life free of the dreaded black pox.

I liked this officer, I guess because his kind had worked their way up from a nobody, such as myself, to officer material, much the same as other officers who had finally made the transition from lowly ratings to then be able to command men with some degree of hands-on knowledge and humanity.

This same medical officer performed an operation of me in Vung Tau harbour when I had an abscess that was giving me pure misery. I had said to the chief:

"I need to go to the sickbay cause I have this pain that's giving me grief and has done for about a week, it's just gotten worse and nothing I take eases it."

"You give me a pain Bruhwiller and nothing I take eases it either, so double away smartly and get it seen to."

Double away smartly was it? I hated that from as far back a recruit school. "Double away smartly lad." Over and over until it was cemented into my psyche, and still is to this day.

"I'll double away smartly chief but I might slip and fall somewhere on this vomit ridden ship."

"Fuck off smart arse," was all he said.

The sickbay was a clean place of solitude and I wondered why I hadn't put my hand up to be a *sick berth attendant*, although they were unfairly labelled queers, much the same as the *steward* rating.

The medical officer took one look at my swollen face, then looked into my mouth and declared the wisdom tooth had to come out, now.

Down we went with a couple of attendants to a little enclosed compartment much the same as what I could only describe as the ship's morgue, obviously specially designed for a ship's war dead. There I was given two injections to numb the pain. When they didn't take he administered another two, and with the two attendants holding me down he went to work to cut around the bastard tooth hoping to get a better grip. Still the painkillers didn't work, hence the only alternative was to grab another two men to pin me to the chair and away he went with a maniacal look in his eyes.

The puss and blood and smell were just putrid I believe. I had fainted by this and had missed the pleasantries. When I came around shortly after the pain was gone, the attendants were gone and the officer was talking to me as if I had been wounded on the front line.

It took me days to recover with my mates saying I was in a bloody good fight with my swollen face and blood continually trickling out the corner of my mouth.

"Yeah, no big deal," I lied.

~~~~~~~~~~~~~~~~~~~

Vung Tau harbour was one of the most picturesque places I have seen, also extremely busy with heavy movement to and from the shoreline. Soldiers, fully laden landing barges, choppers buzzing around especially on the lookout for would be antagonists on Vung Tau ridge and in the harbour itself, since our ship was a prize target for the enemy, no doubt.

The noise was deafening with the roar of engines and percussion grenades to ward off enemy frogmen looking to mine the flotilla moored there. I loved the smell of the diesels' smog and the odours emulating from the port itself, so my first thought was to see my commanding officer and ask for shore leave to see my brother Michael, posted to logistics in Vung Tau itself. He gave me a negative excuse relating to the deaths of three brothers during the last Great War due to them being billeted on the same ship, which was sunk with all hands. It was also decreed to involve any direct relatives from any armed forces being in any war zones together.

So I went anyway.

I wore overalls and a peaked cap I had swiped, grabbed some important looking baggage and hopped a barge thinking no more of it. The place was so busy I was sure I wouldn't be missed for a few hours.

Once on shore I had no fear and no real idea where to go except the nearest bar, only out of curiosity I assure you, since I had no money to speak of and no condoms. It was never my intention to risk having my dick drop off.

The place was like a wide-open wild west show with non-stop partying, or so it seemed to me at the time. Kings Cross didn't have a patch on this. Endless bars with, what appeared to be American names, prolifically displayed welcoming you into their premises and into their girls: ally and enemy alike. Yes, that's right, some Viet Cong senior personnel were known to take some R and R there as well.

I do remember The Beachcomber bar and the beach nearby, the Back Beach, but I was only told the name of this beach some time after when returning home with the army boys.

I quickly had a look around, although I didn't make it to the Australian logistics area seeing I was way out of my depth here.

With my head down and looking busy, along with the rest of the local population there at the time, I ducked into a sheltered drink stand at the same instant two enemy on a small motor cycle came ripping up the street firing a pistol and then launching a grenade into the doorway of a bar, only to miss it completely with the bomb rolling harmlessly into an alleyway before exploding. Everyone dove for cover before a couple of military police on patrol opened up on the culprits, missing them completely. I believe no one was injured in the assault, this time.

Some time later my brother explained to me that these two foe on the bike were probably amateurs, acting independently, unaware their own comrades could have been in the firing line. To some extent Vung Tau had been off-limits for combat operations.

As a result of all the commotion, I bolted to a barge to get to the safety of my ship, also not wanting to be in trouble if I was discovered missing. One shouldn't disobey direct orders in a war zone, so I told no one of my little adventure for fear of being hung from the yardarm at dawn.

Let me say though, the scent of this beautiful country, with all of its ghosts and past violence, remains with me to this day.

Back on board all was well and we drank, gambled and talked rubbish until it was time to leave with a much lighter load than when we arrived.

The night before we set sail I, along with a couple of others, were sent down to the bowels of this great old ship to check for leaks along the huge shafts that propelled her. You could say we were a few inches from the ocean outside with steel and rivets just separating us, when BANG, inches from our head a percussion grenade exploded. Well, we all pissed our pants and moved upward as quickly as possible along with the leading seaman who was supervising us and whom I later thought should have been familiar with such things. He told me he had been down there before, yet had never heard such a frightening sound as on this occasion. You could have sworn an enemy explosion had holed the ship.

An *advocate* told me many years later this story had been used to death when veterans had been applying for recognition of their ailments. I'll tell you now, I had logged this many years prior to our conversation.

We left Vung Tau early on a mist with a mesmerising sunrise breaking the horizon upon a most innocuous sea.

Who would think a few miles away inland, death was playing its treacherous fiddle?

All was calm into the South China Sea a day out into our return journey when suddenly we were set upon by the most hawkish typhoon seen for some years, I was told later.

We were ordered to secure everything movable including advising the pongos who had decided to return with us and not fly home, that they were in for the ride of their lives, us included, since we were new to this ominous sea as well.

Furthermore, it has to be remembered the ship was way under capacity as far as weight and ballast were concerned, due obviously to its cargo being offloaded. This ship, previously an aircraft carrier, was sitting on the water much the same as a cork bobbing around in a bathtub.

Our skipper headed directly into the jaws of the beast, and where were we? Securing ourselves to the upper flight deck and having the ride of our lives, including more army boys than I would have imagined. I guess after their time on the front line of combat that this was pure pleasure and a place to let off steam and maybe a place to wash away their previous turbulent twelve months; mine as well. I was to discover during our return journey some of their misgivings, doubts and disappointments at a world gone to shit in a shopping bag.

The cleansing monster waves were something to behold as they washed over the deck and us while we squawked and yahooed as loud as we could. We swore along with the pongos and generally made a puerile time of it, until we were told to get below decks. Although we were quite safe in our positions way back from the bow it was decided that the navy was coming back with its full complement, and with all the soldiers entrusted to it.

Many of the army lads had issues and showed us photos of their girls from home and from Vietnam, along with photos of war dead, villages burned, the odd very real atrocity perpetrated by the enemy and some porn photos from the bars where they drank and played.

I asked one sad looking bloke why he didn't want to fly home as many others had; he imparted this comment to me:

"You know mate, I just wanted to take my time going home so I could get my shit together. My girl fucked me off and I hear the welcome home is a little troubling."

I guess he meant the home ports were more welcoming than the airports where some obtuse peace lovers were happy to swear and spit on you when you left the terminal. Baby killers and rapists they would have you believe and as I have said, a bunch of hateful and hostile ingrates was the only way to describe these cretins, while the genuine hippy was just that, harmless and loving who yearned for a better world, along with us.

We kept our distance from the pongos on this return journey because they seemed so far removed from us, unlike the guys we took up there.

Is this what war does to its survivors? And they out-smoked us, out-drank us, out-gambled us, out-swore us and wandered about lost at times. We didn't want to compete with them. They had won by coming home on a slow boat from China.

My schoolmates were still at school and not yet accomplished in their high school studies.

Sydney's *first voyage to South Vietnam, escorted by HMAS* **Melbourne**, *HMAS* **Duchess** *and HMAS* **Parramatta***, began on 27 May 1965. For* **Sydney's** *crew, the trip meant the chance to both establish routines for a logistic task, the like of which had not been undertaken by the navy for twenty years, and to gain an understanding of the risks facing their ship in hostile waters. In the years to come, the run to Vung Tau and back became an increasingly speedy and smooth operation. Nevertheless, each voyage required a great deal of hard work, particularly during the loading and unloading phase of the operation.*

In its role as the 'Vung Tau Ferry', HMAS Sydney brought together men from two distinct cultures: the army and the navy. In the days before she sailed from Australia, Sydney would be loaded with soldiers and their equipment. Crew members would be detailed to act as 'sea daddies' to groups of soldiers, helping them to get their bearings on board ship, showing them where to keep their gear and how to sling their hammocks – a novel, and often unwelcome, mode of sleeping for most soldiers. Apart from the unfamiliarity with shipboard life, or indeed with the ways of the navy, the soldiers often found Sydney to be uncomfortable, particularly in tropical waters when the heat below decks was intense.

During loading and unloading, when Sydney and her escort ships were anchored off Vung Tau, their crews were prepared to counter any attacks launched from shore. The ship's divers carried out constant patrols, checking hulls and cables while armed sentries stood on deck with orders to fire on suspicious movements in the water. She performed in her role as 'Vung Tau ferry' very effectively, safely transporting thousands of troops to and from Vietnam along with thousands of tonnes of cargo and equipment.

By 1972, when Australia's involvement in Vietnam ended, Sydney had carried 16,000 army and RAAF personnel to Vung Tau on 24 ferry runs and had made a 25th trip to Vietnam to deliver and pick-up military equipment. Every voyage took between 10 and 12 days in each direction, a time during which soldiers heading for Vietnam were given hours of physical training and prepared for the year that they would have to spend as combatants in a war zone. For those on the return voyage after their twelve-month tour of duty, the passage to Australia offered a chance to relax, to reflect on their experiences and to prepare themselves for the transition from war to peace. Such a period of reflection was denied to those soldiers who returned home by aircraft, leaving Vietnam and being home within 10 hours. Although many Vietnam veterans recall being ignored upon their return to Australia, this was not the case for those who returned with their battalions on board HMAS Sydney.

This article is reproduced with permission from the Department of Veterans' Affairs, Australia and their Vietnam War articles.

3ʳᵈ *Chapter*

BECOMING AN ABLE SEAMAN

'Life is fired at us point blank.'

Jose` Ortega y Gasset

I returned from this voyage somewhat shell-shocked, thanks to having experienced a dogmatic disintegration of my own behaviour compared to my good Christian upbringing. Nothing to do with war wounds of course. I'll leave that to the blokes who fought on the front line. My experience so far though was something best left to adults, not children. Do I think any differently now? Can I say here, anyone who pushes children into adulthood before their time is guilty of negligence, including children portrayed as adults to sell any commodity, and parents 'exhibiting' their five year olds in pageants. Let children be children for a long a possible without the competitive soul-destroying fluff, pomp and ceremony so prolific in today's society. They will have plenty of time to bow before the gaffer.

Sure it made men of us. Men who had a completely different and unhealthy perspective on life who were protected and outside civilian law to a degree: gamblers, excessive drinkers and smokers, fornicators, foul-mouthed rebels and non-conformists in the greater scheme of things, shielded in a cocooned environment we only answered to our masters and no one else.

And yes, I knew many during my time who would blow their pay the first night on leave then spend the following fortnight bludging off shipmates and living free on their ship or base.

The navy's *wet canteens* were often a free-for-all at a duty-free discount where we could drown ourselves in grog then climb into cars or onto motorcycles only to kill or maim ourselves, and maybe others. Such was the case not only with my best man-to-be at my impending wedding, but also with a good mate, Andy, who lost his life after a night out in Melbourne: more on that later though.

Onward forty years at a navy reunion, I witnessed two old sailors performing the *dance of the flaming arseholes* naked, where one would stuff a rolled up newspaper up one's bum and light it, then the protagonist would run around at a great rate of knots to avoid being burnt; the one who managed to outrun the flames the longest was declared the winner. It was pathetic and funny seeing these old blokes, whose dicks had been replaced with something resembling a button on an overcoat, grunting around the bar drunk as lords. It undoubtedly did make men of us!

~~~~~~~~~~~~~~~~~~~

Frankston, forty miles from Melbourne is the training base for the more senior recruits entering the navy. It was also our new home while we completed our courses to become able seamen trained in our fields of operation: mine being engineering as an unqualified diesel mechanic, nevertheless, with years on the job you were well versed in the running and maintenance of diesel engines and generators without obtaining a trade certificate. Obviously it was up to the individuals to improve themselves while serving, although most didn't.

My father joined the navy through this base, H.M.A.S. Cerberus, some eighteen years prior after he finished his apprenticeship with the New South Wales railways as a 'fitter and turner'. His ranking was that of a petty officer (the equivalent to an army sergeant), however, due to mum's ill health he was discharged on compassionate grounds.

While we were being educated in the operation of power plants, our life was mostly free from the drudgery of naval training except for a weekly parade ground formation, and an inspection of our dormitory rooms and facilities more regularly.

It was during one of these inspections I discovered an enemy within when I found my gear had been tampered with. The officer told my immediate superior to get me into my shared quarters and explain what the hell I thought I was doing here and was I on a holiday. It wasn't a question.

"What the fuck happened here?" I said.

They could see by my shock I was not responsible for the mess, which consisted of a few things strewn about, bed pulled down and after-shave sprayed over some personal belongings including my radio.

"What's the problem here sailor?"

"Buggered if I know sir."

"Who have you been fighting with?" said the officer.

"Not sure, sir."

"Not sure?"

I wasn't sure, but I had an idea it was someone I called a poofter at the wet canteen: him and all of his likewise companions, because I didn't like their bum-sniffing holier-than-thou attitude. I didn't say anything at the time, so I just let it go.

"I'll keep an eye out sir."

"Make sure you do sailor, I don't want any more of this going on, now double away smartly lad."

There it was again, 'double away smartly'!

"Can I just walk sir cause I have a crook knee?" I lied.

"Go to the sick bay then."

"I will sir," I lied again.

The drudgery of school continued only to be broken by the ability to drink beer, talk bullshit, play cards and generally make nuisances of ourselves, beginning at the base then all the way into Melbourne and back again.

I became quite prolific with my poker face and ability to skull copious amounts of beer better than anyone else due to my lack of a gullet. Pour it down to win bets and play poker to win even more money, not bad for a skinny seventeen year old. It won me friends and enemies alike, although not too many of the latter except the odd lad I may have offended with a quick wit and big mouth while drinking to excess.

Drinking had become an issue on and off the base with accidents a regular occurrence on the road from Melbourne to the base after a night out, and because I was not mobile at this particular time I relied on some mad mates for a ride.

It culminated in the base commander getting a hold of a few movies for us to view in the cinema, titled Highway 66, Highway of Death and Mechanised Death. As with the movies and photos of sexually transmitted diseases these were real shockers. Actual road carnage I had never seen before, more so than some combat footage so prolifically viewed at the time, and other harrowing war footage not seen by the general public.

Funny how the images of bits and pieces of adults, children and babies slaughtered in metal coffins by trucks, drunks and other ill-fated your-time-is-up occurrences have a numbing effect on most viewers. It seems to be relegated to the deep, dark recesses on the mind never to resurface except under exceptional circumstances, as was the case with my friend Andy.

I had driven with him occasionally to the city and a funnier bloke you would never meet. He was the cheeky bastard who shaved his head first at recruit school and got into trouble because it wasn't regulation, always the prankster and always laughing. The joker who bought a cheap beat up old trail bike, repaired it to running order and let us all demolish it in the base car park by trouncing it through mud; generous to the bone, but always in trouble. He once told the duty officer on the front gate, when we were there at midnight to scrub and clean the area as punishment for some other minor infringement to their law, that he treated the base cat better than he did the sailors. He was yelled down and in a world of shit for his insubordination. Later the cat had an 'accident' when it had the misfortune of stumbling into the furnace, which was kept burning in the boom gate office during the colder months.

He was initially blamed, although I knew he didn't do it. I was there when another sailor took offence to the cat's coddled status on the base. No, it didn't burn to death: the cat jumped out like a shot and escaped with only minor injuries. The officer locked the base down until a more senior officer revoked the order and told his junior subordinate to grow up. Andy was not charged, but a severe warning was issued deeming the cat off-limits.

Prior to Andy's accident we had been introduced to the White Ensign Club in Melbourne, otherwise known as *Screamers* to the many homesick and lost sailors visiting the shores of this city, and a place to let their hair down, similar to our own displaced status.

If Vung Tau was a wild west show Screamers was its sister town in every sense of the analogy, where music, girls, gambling and outrageous behaviour was commonplace.

The premises even had small cubicles where one could lay their weary, drunken head down on a small bed after a night of frivolous fun. Also, one had the ability to slip a girl into this small space much the same as a toilet cubicle, although a little bigger of course, all for a small fee and a towel provided.

Drunken cooks and *stokers* (the engineering branch) were the most outrageously behaved doing 'the dance of the flamers' and spitting sputum into each other's glass of beer then drinking it in one gulp: not to mention vomit as well. These blokes, as cheerful as ever, were also into the habit of other playful activities including the sabotage of bottles of beer with their urine. I suffered at their hands, once.

Girls were plentiful and ready to become sailors' girlfriends with an eventual view to marriage. I guess this has a ring to it for those who have heard of such things, since many young ladies did want to retreat from their dead-end dreary lives, and what better way than to travel and live in different exotic locations at the expense of the government? Resorts like the inner western suburbs of Sydney. They considered anywhere was an improvement over Melbourne, however, little did they know their life would come to an abrupt standstill with a couple of kids in tow, stuck in a small unit and fucking other sailors when hubby was away: what a shit-fight, with many a tear and mendacious marriage collapse in the offing.

Many young men fell in love at Screamers including myself. She was a cute blond petite thing we would describe as a *spinner*. What is a spinner you may well ask? The subtlest way to describe this terminology would be to say that she was small enough to position her on one's dick while laying on one's back then spinning her around until you came: a somewhat exaggerated delusion.

Anyway, apart from being stunning and well-dressed, I concluded from our conversation she was from a good family and well educated; nevertheless we got drunk, got into one of these little cubicles and had a good old time. She seemed a bit more experienced than I would have assumed for such a pretty, attractive young girl.

She then showered and left me to sleep it off with a promise to see me the next night.

By the time I got back there late the following evening due to a drinking session in the city with a few mates, she had hooked up with someone else. It was on when I tried to break into their space only to be told to fuck off in no uncertain terms by her, and her new bloke. I was gutted and called her and the guy for everything until the doormen threw me out.

A couple of days later I discovered she had given me the crabs.

Not to be outdone though, one of my mates had sex with a damsel he had picked up there and came to us saying she was, or had been, a virgin because she had bled on him.

We, by this time, had wizened up to our naivety and told him she was such a slut he had probably fucked her while she was having her period.

"No way," he said. "She's a bloody virgin for sure."

"Mate, if she's hanging around here she's no virgin."

"Bullshit guys, you're just jealous cause she's a real good looker," he argued.

"You probably just knocked a couple of scabs off her box," I said, being bitter, stupid and unthinking. He then just up and left us to continue his romance until she dumped him when a better offer came along.

On the positive side, some older recruits from our base were a bit more astute in their choice of girls, with one telling us he called his new girlfriend *ramblin' rose,* like the rose bush, because he said:

"She wasn't any good in a bed, but rooted well against a wall."

At this particular time rumours began to circulate regarding a number of our intake that had left us for other parts of this, and other worlds, such as our mate from recruit school, Charlie, who had hung himself over some piece of fluff while serving on his first ship. The cooks found him hanging from a beam in the galley when they commenced work early one morning.

Others had been discharged medically unfit, permanently injured due to life's austerity via incidents and accidents, or killed outright on our roads.

It must be remembered that we had lost contact with most of our original intake owing to the different fields of operations we had entered, and as it does eventually, news began to trickle through in relation to our comrades-in-arms with whom we had initially joined the service.

On a lighter note, my crab issue became perplexing due to shaving the offending genitals, and then having my accommodation and clothing fumigated, along with the others who shared our donger. I then had to name the offending carrier, which I didn't, hoping the next guy(s) who fucked her would cop a dose as well, such was my thoughtlessness. I should have identified her so the navy could have contacted her parents and told them what a slut they had hatched. Then again she probably would have blamed *me* for giving them to her.

I was the joke of the day with comments on how to rid yourself of the little bastards: beer and sand rubbed vigorously into your groin so the crabs get pissed and stone each other to death. Or get a mirror and hold it below your balls; when the crabs see a fresh set of jewels they will jump onto the mirror and slip off, then you can stomp on 'em: funny bastards, my shipmates.

So it went on for some time with incidents and accidents both of a humorous and serious nature. One being the night we spent at an up-market bar in the heart of Melbourne where a middle aged man asked us all up to his room to watch the boxing on television, so in our naivety we all agreed. There would have been eight or ten of us and a biggish girl who was with me. Not fat, just well proportioned, yet very appealing and she thought the sun shone out of my bum. I guess she was only human!

As time progressed, when we were all drunk and crashed out, she stripped off and climbed on top of me with half a dozen mates asleep and strewn over the same ample bed. She had her way and I had mine, then she climbed off and crashed too. I woke with my mate Joe wiping himself after a quick shower and complaining the towel he had used must have been the same towel with which she had wiped herself after sex. We all just fell about laughing, then crashed again after a couple more beers.

I awoke later to discover this gentleman, who had invited us to his room, latching onto my family jewels, with this girl still asleep beside me and no one else in sight. I just bitch slapped him away from me and woke her; we then dressed and left with his bottle of scotch proclaiming we would perform a tap dance on his head if he moved. I later thanked my buddies for leaving us there within this predator's clutches.

They were all determined to return to the scene of the crime and castrate him, just to be kind, mind you.

Around this time I had an idea as to the identity of my antagonist at the base after a couple of other incidents had occurred, yet nothing too drastic, just annoying.

At the monthly dance held in our gymnasium I got drunk enough to front this sailor from my intake at recruit school. I couldn't really believe that some prick who had gone through what we all went through would get it in their head to scurry around like a rat in the night instead of just coming out and saying I had offending him in some minor way, and settle it there and then.

After the dance I followed him up a flight of stairs and when he reached the top I was there right behind him.

"What the fuck's hanging out of you mate?" I challenged.

He then turned and said to me:

"You're a cunt."

"You'd know that how? Your mum's shown hers to every bastard, so I suppose that's how." I answered for him.

With that he took a swing at me, lost his footing in his inebriated state and slipped right past me only to tumble down twenty odd concrete steps. Was he damaged goods when he finally bounced off the last step? Big time and I hadn't lifted a finger.

When I got to him I said:

"Sorry for saying that about your mum......she's probably only had three fucks in her life, the army, navy and the air force."

With that I left him there only to be told, and eventually seeing, he had really banged himself up and was in a bad way. No more problems though, and because there wasn't a collaborating witness to support him he didn't say a word or accuse me of any wrongdoing.

Andy, having been a confidant in the aforementioned matter was with me, along with a few others on the night in question, and had wanted to urinate on the culprit there and then, but good sense prevailed. And who could have blamed us after the trouble he caused with the ongoing investigation into his petty misbehaviour? It was a real pain in the arse for many in the block who had been questioned over the incidents.

We had a laugh or two over many things in our time, Andy and I, especially when we were hand-picked for payroll duty and given .45 calibre automatic pistols to guard the base cash reserves when it came to paying us our lowly wage.

Andy being a mad bastard, and I following close behind, were taken out to a firing range with a few others to practice our shooting prowess. Well, we hit everyone else's target beside us and not our own. At fifteen to twenty feet, approximately six metres, I still couldn't hit a full man size figure with the ugliest head I had ever seen. I wanted to blow it off his shoulders, but to no avail. These American .45s were heavy and cumbersome to the likes of my small stature, and Andy kept calling me *sparky* because the gun hung so low on my hip the sparks would fly from its barrel as it touched the ground: a slight exaggeration. I've heard the term sparky used to describe the short-arse recruits inducted into the police services nowadays, then I figure Andy used it first though.

So, on an early morning pick up of money from a major bank in Melbourne we were robbed while Andy and I were inside. Three others had just walked outside with the cash when up from behind a car stopped, three armed masked men held up the boys, including a chief who was in charge, and took the cashbox. We inside just glimpsed the robbery and doing it by the numbers we took three bullets out of one pocket, then took our magazine out of the other pocket and proceeded to load the three bullets into the empty magazine, then slam home the clip into the base of the handle; pull back the slide to engage the bullet into the chamber then switch off the safety and stick our heads out the door, by which time the cops had arrived: it took us about three minutes I guess. Useless bloody tits we were.

Why all the tedious procedure? We weren't allowed to carry loaded weapons.

We all thought it was an inside job planned by some desperate sailor who had done his dough to some criminal element, and to pay off his debts he set up this heist. It went so smoothly it even surprised the police, who probably had a cut coming to them as well, such as it was then with police corruption in Melbourne and Sydney.

Andy died following a night out in town while driving his Chrysler back to base with a mate. We were about a minute or two behind him on a dark misty road in mid-winter, and thanks to a fait accompli I had decided to travel with another mate on that particular evening. We had all been drinking and were generally in good spirits, since our engineering course was coming to an end and the next step was to be our first *draught* (transfer to a ship or base) as able seamen.

We stopped to see if we could help not really knowing who or what it was, such was the condition of the wreck. The only tell-tale sign it was one of us was a lonely sailor's cap lying in the middle of the road. I picked it up and turned it over to discover Andy's name on the inside rim. There was nothing left of Andy to speak of, such is the consequence when you hit a tree at great speed. His mate was thrown clear and survived, just, with permanent injuries.

My guardian again? I began to wonder…. again.

Andy's guardian was on leave that night I suppose; still he had a good farewell from us all, never to be forgotten, as you can see here in my story.

✂ ✂ ✂ ✂ ✂ ✂ ✂ ✂ ✂ ✂ ✂ ✂ ✂ ✂ ✂ ✂ ✂ ✂

I met Anne through a friend in the city not long before I left Cerberus where so much had happened in so little time.

She was a country girl much more mature than I, working for a big bank in Melbourne, educated, from a good family and just a little older than myself.

This is where I became unstuck when it came to love. She was a virgin, blond and attractive and I fell in love with her, and eventually her family, from a little town out west called Dimboola, some two hundred miles from Melbourne.

And this is where I had become torn between the outback and the ocean, and longed to spend more time there than on the water. It just goes back to being too young to enlist for any great length of time before you can reconcile where life is taking you. Nowadays, one can enlist, still at seventeen with the consent of the parents, for only one year *behind* enemy lines to see if the military life will suit you: a somewhat more sensible approach to recruitment.

I had only been with Anne for a short time when I was transferred out to my new ship, H.M.A.S. Stalwart at Garden Island down from Kings Cross once again; hence I made it my arduous and unpleasant task to regularly travel the most treacherous road in the nation between Sydney and Melbourne just to be with her. Prior to an expressway being built this road had the most number of fatalities in the country, and every time I ventured onto it I not only took my life into my own hands, I was also to witness and experience some of the most horrific smashes you could happen upon.

Without going into too many details I will tell you of a couple of incidents I/we encountered on our regular twelve hundred mile (around 2,000k/m) return journeys.

A couple of us had chipped in to buy an old bomb in Melbourne, since there were always sailors ready for a trip interstate for whatever reason, and half way up on an earlier trip in this old Austin A40 the bonnet flew off, then the car shit itself. Here we were in the middle of nowhere in the heart of winter freezing our socks off, when along came this old Morris Minor and offered us a lift. Two of us climbed aboard with our third co-traveller refraining for entering this other heap. We were desperate though, so off we went before we noticed he was as drunk as a fool with his girlfriend not too far behind. It was a nightmare with him wanting to fight her and/or us, swearing, swerving and asking her for a 'root or a head job'. And on it went until we reached civilisation, where we jumped out with our gear and kicked the side of his car as I said to her:

"Get a new bloke cause you'll be dead by this time tomorrow if you stay with that dickhead".

"Yeah, fuck off," they both said, and drove erratically onward to their doom, we hoped.

On another trip not long after, we were hitching a ride to Sydney and along came this imbecile who wanted to kill us for sport. I didn't know my companion very well on this occasion, nevertheless we jumped from the car first chance we had, but the bastard stopped and pulled out a rifle. We scattered and hid off the road behind trees until car headlights could be seen in the distance. Being a dark wet night we were safe we thought, and had even managed to grab our bags as we scurried out of his car. He just laughed and yelled out he was only shitting us, then drove off before the other car reached our position.

In the morning we spotted him entering a pub well over two hundred miles from where we escaped his perhaps murderous intensions. We had hitched another ride to this town and then my companion just marched into the pub and beat the devil out of this fool. I was mesmerised, since it happened so quickly, and when it was all over bar the shouting we took his car and dumped it a way up the road, threw his keys into the bush and hitched another ride to Sydney.

An incident, or should I say an accident I remember vividly occurred one late summer evening miles from nowhere when a Toyota Troop carrier outfitted as a camper came tearing up behind us and without slowing, veered out to overtake our car without so much as checking the oncoming traffic. He cut us off to pull in before a semi-trailer could wipe him out, just a little too late though. The truck sideswiped his troopy and took off his rear view mirror along with his arm, which happened to be hanging out of his window. The arm hit our windscreen along with copious amounts of blood but didn't cause any damage, to us. We stopped to assist the loon; nevertheless he bled to death while we all stood around looking stupid. We did attempt to stem the bleeding along with a nurse who had also stopped to help the poor soon-to-be deceased.

We had travelled this route on numerous occasions because we had girlfriends, wives and family we were desperate to see. I was laughed at many times with the guys saying Anne must have been the best screw in the world.

I didn't take offence, since it was the nature of the beast in all of us, and yes, I liked being with her to such a degree I had asked her to marry me.

My reasoning was such that by now it was not so much...was I really in love? Being loved and being accepted by a fine girl and a fine family from the country was all that mattered. Immaturity personified.

~~~~~~~~~~~~~~~~~~~~~

Eventually, back in Sydney, we sailed for the Philippines in the new fleet maintenance ship, H.M.A.S. Stalwart, on a calm early morning tide. We departed a glistening Sydney Harbour, which made me reminisce about Vung Tau's port and its beauty. In my mind's eye it left me with an artist's impression of how Sydney's shoreline would have been when it was first settled.

Let me say here that the Stalwart, being a new addition to the fleet, had many senior exchange personnel from England with an old world mentality regarding war time rules, or any naval rules and traditions for that matter. 'Hang him from the yardarm'; 'twenty lashes at dawn on the foredeck with all personnel to witness'; 'keelhaul the blighter' and 'walk the plank you scoundrel', if you were to breach any of their commands or behave unceremoniously toward their ideal and their complete totalitarianism.

There was a constant murmuring among the crew and when we were finally let ashore all hell seemed to break loose with bad behaviour at an optimum......letting off steam no doubt. To this day I can't really put my finger on it. Nevertheless, within the following few months I would be in a military corrective establishment for assault and insubordination.

We had determined their harshness towards us while undertaking sea trials up and down the east coast, although we did have fun with the nurses from various hospitals when we berthed at ports along our coastline.

Not to cast dispersions on these wonderful, yet willing girls back then, but they were employed in the actual wards immediately upon their securing a job, unlike today where they are college graduates and lack the easy going nature of the nurses of yesteryear. Is this a good thing? I suppose it is, maybe.

We had only to call in or phone to see if a shift was finishing and they would meet us at the hospital or a bar close by, then off we would go sometimes finding ourselves on a beach or in a cave close to the water with a fire and a plentiful supply of food and grog.

~~~~~~~~~~~~~~~~

Olongapo, in the Philippines, was another wild west show across a bridge and into a one street town, the one street you would stay on if you valued your life, with bars and brothels on either side. Yet no one seemed to get past the first watering hole because they would hoist the name of your ship outside their premises before it berthed (the Sydney Bar, The Stalwart Bar, et cetera.) and there you stayed until dawn, or return to your ship by midnight, since a curfew was then enforced until six a.m.

This place came and went in a blur with bad behaviour, girls, outlandish shows, drugs, Americans from their Subic Bay base, violence and communists ready to murder you if the 'butterfly boys' didn't get you first.

The leading story at the time was two American sailors were found hanging upside down under the bridge with their genitalia shoved into their mouths, probably inflicted by communist insurgents during curfew: a reminder all was not well here.

Butterfly boys were what the local girls referred to if *you* were seeing more than one of their competitors from another bar, then you were labelled the offending butterfly boy. Ironically, this was considered adultery and a sin in their eyes, however, the word among us sailors that a butterfly boy was a pimp who watched over his girls, and would use his butterfly knife on you for sport if you crossed him or his ladies. These knives were at least a foot long (30 centimetres) with the blade hidden between two grips and when flipped open would reveal a razor sharp cutter the same length as the handle: a nasty piece of work.

The movie Priscilla, Queen of the Desert, gave you a taste of the robust achievements these girls were capable of with ping-pong balls. Eggs, cigars and the ability to retrieve coins thrown onto the stage with their womanly charms being a feat within itself, especially when one of the crowd superheated his coin with a cigarette lighter then threw it onstage where it was swooped on by one of the ladies. All hell broke loose as she screamed in pain with two culprits running out of the bar pursued by two butterfly boys wielding their knives.

Outside, one of the sailors picked up an iron pipe and split open the skull of one of his knife wielding assailants. He went down and was dead before he hit the ground, the other vanished.

Sex was cheap as was life, with the Reaper hanging over you if you fucked the wrong clap infested girl or one of her opponents operating in another bar, or you fucked with her pimp, fucked with the curfew and the communists or fucked with illicit drugs. Abstinence and common sense was the best line of defence, which no one practiced as frustrations boiled over.

As for the bloke who defended himself, he was never identified, although he told me about it later when an investigation was taking place into a body being found in an alley. He never spoke of it again and neither did I for that matter.

Next stop on the return leg was Bunbury in Western Australia. A small coastal port well south of the capital Perth and as quaint a place you would ever hope to visit, until the Stalwart arrived.

We took over the town on an early afternoon mid-week and as we wandered the streets the schoolgirls were coming out wanting to chat to us. From there it was grog and mayhem. The police were called to numerous emergencies involving parents concerned for their daughters' welfare, underage drinking, homes being invaded by sailors wanting to acquaint themselves with the locals, and their daughters. Plus, the pubs exhausted their beer stock, much to the disgust of the boys, so rioting and destruction were prolific.

An incident that shocked even the most hardened of us happened to an elderly couple who had invited a couple of the boys into their home for a chat and a snack, while they were inebriated, to try and sober them up, no doubt. Their reward was one of these dopes bit the head off their pet budgie.

The following day the ship was ordered from port and the captain was told he was never to set foot in their town again, along with his ship, of course.

I can honestly say today that I never misbehaved on this trip, maybe due to the fact I had a girl I respected, and since achieving my diesel rating I could see my life turning around.

Unfortunately this was not to be.

Back in Sydney there was time for leave and reconnecting with loved ones. I had recently taken over a lease from my brother on a unit he had rented at North Bondi, on the fringe of Tamarama Bay to be more precise, so a few of us chipped in to keep the place as our getaway from the humdrum of navy life.

Many good times resulted from us having a taste of civilian life in this place, which had a view to die for, and I'm sure to this day there would be more than a few who hold fond memories of this little piece of Bondi heaven.

It was only a small block with six units, hence we became friendly with all the neighbours, and because it was now in my name it was the first place Anne and I had to ourselves when we finally married. Our friendships with a few of these neighbours remain to this day.

We were all at a party for a new arrival at the units who had recently arrived from interstate. As it turned out she was a nymphomaniac in the true sense of the word, and when her husband went to bed early she was on my mate's old boy and giving him a blowjob with all of us sitting around in the lounge room. We all thought it was as funny-as-a-feed-of-arse (a coarse term for hilarious) and she went on to fuck a few more of the crew over time while the hubby was aware of her infidelities. It stumped us, after all, we had seen a thing or two to date. She had even said to us her husband didn't mind, and that she had also sent him on a course to improve his disposition and personality. A nice quiet type of bloke we all agreed, but a loser in the woman stakes. I remember a few of their own sports team members came for a visit from their home state only to give her some as well. She was an attractive woman though, with a great personality.

It was during this unconstrained civilian life we were ordered to set sail for manoeuvres and more sea trials up north. Before we left we had asked if we were to load up with our full kits or to just take a steaming kit along with us. This was an ordinary request when if at sea for longer periods and visiting ports we would have to take dress clothes, civvies and full kits as well.

We were emphatically told it was steaming kit only for this short trip: work overalls, shipboard cloths and personal items, since we would only be gone for a week or two with no ports of call.

Around three days out at sea off Queensland's north coast we were instructed to have full kit musters in, of course, alphabetical order. Our immediate English superior, a lieutenant commander by the name of Carpenter, along with his chief, unfortunately for us from the same mould, concocted this scheme to flex their authority, no doubt.

My comment to him was:

"Chief, you told us that a steaming kit was all that was required this trip, and now we're supposed to have a kit muster with *all* our kit. What's the go?"

"Just do as you're told Bruhwiller."

"No kit here chief, what am I supposed to do?"

"Buy a new kit will be the order," he said.

"Like fuck I will chief. I have witnesses who will tell it loud and clear that a steaming kit was all we would need this trip, and if you think I'm paying out three hundred bucks for a new kit then it ain't gonna happen."

"We'll see sailor. Now fuck off and report to the engineering deck on the double," he ordered.

Up on the engineering level this commander was there waiting for his orders to be carried out when I fronted up to him with the chief.

I stood at attention and saluted.

"Where's your kit sailor?" he asked.

"Here sir. How do you want me, standing up or laying down?"

"What?"

"How do you want me, standing up or laying down?"

On cue this English officer started in on me with such a volley of maledictions until I stepped back, took off my hat and threw it at him. I was subdued by a chief petty officer who was passing by and had witnessed the whole incident, then I was taken to the brig.

No real repercussions from other senior or junior personnel, since it was something that had been brewing for some time and I just happened to be the ass who brought it to a head.

In an incident just prior to my meltdown a sailor had left a razor blade protruding from a tiny bar of soap on a ledge above a shower cubicle, and the inspecting hostile junior officer who had been giving sailors a hard time regarding cleanliness, with inspections to be done over and over again, was caught out and injured. This was an uncalled for exercise by another blow-in foreign officer, because we were well trained in shipboard hygiene and well versed by our immediate superiors regarding our living quarters. The sailor had purposely set up the booby trap to catch this officer's habit of running his fingers over every nook and cranny, culminating in his bleeding profusely when he cut his hand discharging his contentious and repetitive practice.

All hell broke loose with threats and intimidation: death by hanging, keelhauling, no beer ration (just as bad, I assure you), no shore leave and so on until the culprit was located. No one came forward.

As for me, I faced the captain with an officer of my choosing for my defence, and he advised me to say nothing at all. He was going with the defence of *guilty with mitigating circumstances*; a defence I would again use on a regular basis. I guess during my service years to say you were guilty, because you always were, with extenuating circumstances or a softening of the issues, was the best defence one could muster.

My problem this time was I imagined myself in another place on fine beaches, swaying palms, cold beer and making out with my lady, so I didn't say anything at all to anybody, even when questioned by the skipper: not a word, much to the amazement of all on board, myself included. And now a new charge of insubordination stemming from my silence after it was ascertained I hadn't been struck dumb by the hand of God.

I was taken off the ship and put on a bus with other military personnel travelling south, but I was the only one who was to spend time in Holsworthy's Military Corrective Establishment.

I was told by a kindly petty officer who was responsible of delivering others to their destinations that he would turn his back to let me step away from the bus and to keep going, because I didn't want to end up *there*. He said during wartime it had all sorts of killers and mad bastards' haunting the place, and that was just the guards, he joked.

'Just fucking terrific,' I thought.

I couldn't see him wrong in that I assumed he would get into a world of shit if I wandered off. He had reassured me he was not obliged to cuff me, and if I had absconded from the rear of a rest café it was not up to him to pursue me, although he would have to inform the naval police sooner rather than later.

I stayed.

Holsworthy Military Corrective Establishment was some forty miles west of Sydney in a desolate part of the outer limits, set amongst the wilds of government land where military exercises regularly took place with firing ranges, cannon and munitions testing and an assortment of other atrocious, yet necessary practices on how to kill and/or maim your fellow man.

The compound was like a Second World War prison camp, a stalag if you like, with barbed wire fences wrapped around the perimeter and armed guards patrolling the outer confines.

The guarded gateway into the camp was your typical boom set up leading down a driveway to the prisoners' accommodation, external toilet, washing and shower facilities and dining area. An external open television area was provided for our half-hour of viewing pleasure every evening to watch the news.

I was led handcuffed from a military bus to begin my sentence for assault and insubordination and to report to the duty chief warrant officer. A big burly man with ribbons and medals on his chest, who looked me up and down, then told the sailor accompanying me to take off the bloody handcuffs, as he so aptly described them. I guess he thought I was no threat at all; he was right, of course.

He again looked me up and down and said to me in his sandpaper growl:

"What the hell are you here for Bruhwiller, is it?"

"Yes chief." I liked the bloke already in that he seemed the genuine, no bullshit type.

These warrant officers who had worked their way up   through the lowly ranks to end up in this unique limbo, somewhere between a chief petty officer and an officer, had earned the respect of both ranking personnel and senior officers alike.

"Well, what are you here for sailor?"

"My charge sheet says assault and insubordination with mitigating circumstances."

"I've seen the charge sheet Bruhwiller, now I'm asking you why are you here?"

"Because they think I'm a bad bastard chief and they want me punished, I guess."

"You guessed right son," he said. "Who was it you assaulted?"

"A lieutenant commander on the Stalwart."

"What happened?"

I felt he was genuinely interested in my plight, so I told him my story ending with the fact that my hard hat had only grazed the bastard officer's shoulder.

"What was this officer's name?" he asked.

"Carpenter."

"Was that a pommy bastard lieutenant commander Carpenter?"

"It was chief."

"He's a right prick Bruhwiller, but you know that don't you. And that's why you're here, right?"

"Yes chief."

"He was a proper cunt when I was under him, so it seems he hasn't changed his ways. Just an anachronism, a leftover from the old English school where they were god and any infringement to their word was punishable with death by hanging," he joked, I hoped.

I wasn't sure what an anachronism was: I gathered the 'leftover from the old pommy navy' comment was as good an explanation as I needed.

Mind you, while on active service and if we had been in enemy waters it could have been a whole new ball game.

Not to be hung of course, but a lengthy term with hard labour would not have been out of the question, this being the present wartime situation with the inmates I was about to meet.

He took me under his wing, this big, gruff chief warrant officer, nevertheless he left me with a warning not to misbehave, keep my nose clean and do what I had to do because he wouldn't be there all the time, although he did leave orders to others that I was to be treated fairly and nothing more.

My cell was at the end of an open cellblock, not unlike single room mini cabins, that reached out to the outer ambit of the camp; consequently, it was a little more peaceful there on the edge of the camp's activities.

Each cell in our section had a bunk and mattress with a few blankets and sheets, which again had to be made to regulation daily. Also, we had a steel bucket for bodily functions and a steel jug of water with a cup, since we were locked away for at least twelve hours each day.

I was left much to myself during my stay seeing word had come down to leave me be, and as a result I wandered around the camp playing a little soccer and volleyball, keeping a low profile and only breaking out of my shell when we played cards and telling our stories while *not* on the grog, which had become a challenge for me.

I did get to know many inmates and a few considered me blessed to be in such a place with deserters, both American and Australian, conscientious objectors, hard case degenerates, murderers, would be murderers, and there was I, with at least some flimsy protective cloak enveloping me. Some had a few bad intentions, since they saw the camp administrator and me as buddies. Not true, I explained to them and then told them of my situation. I guess they felt their plight, once they interfered with me, would be untenable. Also, there were those who unjustifiably considered I could put in a good word for them, thinking they would get an easy gig from time to time. In their eyes I was almost untouchable, nevertheless we were all on our guard at all times waiting for the sky to fall.

The heads and showers were open affairs and whether it was cold as a witch's tit or as sweaty and hot as a demon's jock we were all there shitting and showering in the wide open spaces with only a roof over our heads and a couple of corrugated iron walls separating us from all the elements.

We would empty our buckets every morning then see to our ablutions within sight of each other at all times.

One dopey bastard thought me his bitch because, in his own words, he considered me 'so cute and blond he wanted to fuck me inside out'.

There it was again from my encounter with the hand-job girl back in recruit school. Cute was I?

I told him I just wanted to be friends, and anyway, I had the clap with ongoing penicillin injections.

"So how about a head job mate?"

"Fuck off," says I.

"A hand job then?" says he.

"I'm not a poof mate."

"Neither am I, Mark."

"So what's wrong with jacking off in your cell of a night," I said, quietly considering that poofs were human and clearly this moron was not.

"That's ok, but there's nothing like the real thing, is there?"

There's nothing like the real thing? Hadn't I also heard that adage before from a sailor who was having it off with a Boogie Street boy before he discovered she was not a she?

Converted to the real thing, hey?

"You really haven't got the clap have you?" he continued.

"Sure have," I lied. "So come back and see me in a month or so because this crap they're injecting is making me feel like shit, and giving me a dose of the shits as well."

I had a couple of mates who had suffered a dose of syphilis, so I was able to describe my symptoms to a tee to keep this reprobate at bay.

I didn't know what the hell I was going to do after that, still I didn't report him either thinking I would have to eventually handle the situation myself.

One day I began talking to a pongo ex-sergeant who seemed to be about ten years my senior; you could tell he was a hard man in the way he held himself and spoke. After I got to know him a little better I ventured into the unknown by asking him:

"So, what's your story mate?"

"Just tried to kill a shithead junior officer who had taken to making a name for himself in the combat zone using my men as gun-fodder, and he had gotten one of the conscripts killed and another one wounded with more to come, I could see it. So I reported him to my C.O. who simply poo-who'd me out of his tent. I took matters into my own hands and pulled a gun on him out in the field and threatened to blow his fucking head off."

"So what happened?" I was excited to think some officers were up themselves for the rent and weren't worth a pinch of dog poo, and one was soon to meet his maker.

"He backed off and reported me, so I said I was going to kill him the next chance I got."

"And?" I asked

"They court-marshalled me and sent me here for eight years."

"Fuck me," I said.

"No thanks."

I also spoke to a transient Australian prisoner who had   killed two of this own in Vung Tau because he said:

"I was as high as a kite and fucked in the head at the time."

He said he didn't remember a thing and now, to this day, he resides in a veteran's home.

I had the impression he knew exactly what he had done, even though he may have been off his head at the time; still, he went on and on about being bullied and harassed by his sergeant. This private metamorphosed into the real killer type when finally pushed to the edge, identical to the movie *Full Metal Jacket* released a few years later, where the bullied recruit snapped, finally killing his contrary sergeant.

The Yank deserters resembled the same young conscripts I had first encountered in the naval cells back in Sydney. The young men who didn't want to be there and were awaiting transfers back to the front line after some sort of servitude.

They again told of the horrors of war and in their words, how no one knew what the fuck they were doing in trying to win it, or why they were there in the first place.

Many believed it was a testing ground to show off the United States' military strength, with new weapons technology being shoved down politicians' throats back home. And with new contracts to be initiated and monetary kickbacks and donations paid to warmongering politicians and the hard-headed general staff, who believed their economy was based on the military war machine, there was no turning back.

Most believed then, and still do, these military strategists along with the C.I.A., assassinated Jack Kennedy because of his pacifist stand on Cuba and Vietnam, his clamp down on corruption and his push for peace with Russia. Some considered this murderous act alone had doomed this once 'saviour' of the free world, the U.S.of A.

Now, being fully entrenched within the arms of pitiful war my fellow prisoners were incensed the 'bleeding hearts', who had forced the cessation of bombing in the north, were in fact the cause of so many more allied casualties. Even enemy casualties may have been less if the sustained bombing had continued, by reason of the communists were being bombed into submission *well before* we capitulated in 1974. As a consequence, when the bombing stopped the casualties on both sides increased dramatically. Astute prisoners were sure of this, as was I. We all just wanted it over and let's face it, commanders didn't like a thinking subordinate, hence many here in confinement were thinkers and conscientious objectors first and conscripted soldiers second.

I also had the impression that the recent Kent State University massacre in Ohio by national guardsmen who opened fire on innocent unarmed students protesting Nixon's invasion of Cambodia was a catalyst in their decision to, not only burn their draft cards, but also to start deserting the military in droves. Killing innocents in a far-off war in one thing, but the killing of one's own countrymen and women by its own military was/is considered most disagreeable and undemocratic, wouldn't you agree?

～～～～～～～～～～～～～～～～～

The breakout was another uncomplicated, yet well-planned derision toward our captors, although I neglected to participate out of pure guilt by way of slapping the face of my well-intentioned chief.

Most were conscripts from the U.S. and Aussie contingents who considered they may have been undetectable in a community that may harbour them. They didn't realise they stood out like sore thumbs with little or no hair, prison uniforms and a look of desperation on their young faces.

Barbed wire cutters smuggled in from God knows where; a few games of volley ball while mapping out the best escape route away from prying eyes; a good lock picker; a stormy rain-drenched night when the guards would spirit themselves away from the elements, and out went about a dozen of them, only to be rounded up and returned within a day: most with cuts, breaks and abrasions to be stitched up and/or set after accidents and resistance. One poor individual was hit by a car a few minutes into his freedom only to be hospitalised with many an injury, never to be returned to the front line. They all thought him a lucky bastard; I wasn't so sure.

Let's not forget the sailors serving time in this prison also, not that I had much to do with them, or anyone for that matter. There were a couple of sex offenders who had escaped the clutches of the law due to their itinerant life in the service, and at long last had been caught after lengthy investigations by both the navy, federal and state police.

These bastards had forgotten the rules of engagement while in *civvy street* with ordinary citizens. They had been picking up women and girls and raping them at knifepoint, being held down by one fool or the other while they carried out their odious deeds.

The fact they could disappear into the night was baffling to the cops, when eventually one of them finally slipped up and was caught in another state, and then under threat of a lifetime of incarceration with hard labour he gave up his accomplice.

It has occurred to me over the years, that with any unsolved crime, the authorities should and probably do take into consideration they could be dealing with these types of transient individuals who have a home away from home in the form of a ship, an overseas base, or a mining camp, where they can disappear back into the holes from which they came.

After two months I had visitors when my mum, dad and much to my surprise, Anne, came to see me. They had been talking to the chief when I arrived at the visitors room and when I strode in my mum began to cry, then I started, followed by Anne. My dad, vatic and strong as always with his first salvo of words then grabbed me and gave me a hug while firmly shaking my hand.

Much had been going on behind my back while I was indisposed, with my mother contacting Naval Headquarters in Canberra and expressed to them in no uncertain terms that I would have been pushed to the very limits to behave in such a way. She had also written off to the Prime Minister and other nobodies to vent her frustration and disappointment in their use of military law on a young boy whom she had never known to lift a finger in anger.

Luckily there had been a sympathetic witness to the whole event from an office opposite to where the incident took place, and he had heard every word. He happened to be a petty officer with whom I was unfamiliar at the time, but was a friend of the family in some way. He had contacted my parents by way of his own folks and told them the story, and informed them of the situation on board this particular ship.

The matter then went to the highest office and within a short period thereafter I was released and returned to my ship, the Stalwart.

Before I left the camp I ambushed my would-be antagonist, still giving me a real hard time, and who I had been avoiding whenever and wherever I could. I had been at my wits end and was close to being abused by my nemesis after not confiding my problem to anyone, although I'm sure the eyes of others had been planted firmly on the situation. You always fought your own battles though.

While in the showers one frosty morning when the air was thick with steam, and with a towel over my head, I flashed past my predator while at the same time slamming his head and face into a misted polished steel mirror while he was shaving. He hit so hard he fell to the floor with smashed teeth and lips, a bloody, broken nose and moaning like the wounded dog he was. He didn't see me and no one else did either, which was the plan. I didn't want to be here any longer than I had to. Sure, they had their suspicions, as did the villain of the story. Finally I let him know I didn't have the clap and was never going to let him in, no matter what.

"I know, but at least I had you in my fantasies," he said later, while still not fully convinced I had it in me to do the damage I did to him. And rightly so, considering he had also tried it on with a few of the others. Revenge and survival was the name of the game, as it is in any prison.

"I'm glad I made someone happy here," I replied sarcastically.

I then said my goodbyes to all my newfound lost souls, and lastly I fronted the chief and thanked him for his time and the trust he had in me, especially when he had let me roam free somewhat.

And while I felt my guardian had been hovering above me all this time, and you do get to contemplate these things while in prison, I couldn't understand why I had to go through all the things that had happened in my life, which had finally led me to this place. Maybe it's a matter of freewill and the choices initiated by me. Is it that God really protects drunks and fools?

~~~~~~~~~~~~~~~~~~~

Back on board the Stalwart now berthed at Garden Island in Sydney, I was welcomed as a type of tittle hero within my department because of my stand, my silence and my mutinous behaviour. ·

The kit musters had been cancelled and things had settled down now the offending officer had been transferred, although his pommy chief mate was still our immediate boss.

I was just starting to settle into a routine again, albeit somewhat vanquished within myself, when out of the blue I was posted to H.M.A.S. Albatross, the navy's fleet air arm base at Jarvis Bay on the New South Wales south coast.

Jarvis Bay was being groomed to sustain our naval fleet in the future; hence I guess my superiors considered I needed to have a change of pace and to discern myself with the heavy and light transport side of the service, combined here into the fleet air arm.

I performed well within these confines and not being at sea was also a bonus in my case, in that I was becoming reacquainted with shore life, which I think the powers-that-be may have believed I was more suited.

During my redeployment to shore I was also reassessed at the apprentice naval base west of Sydney for what reason I'm unsure of to this day, although I think it may have had something to do with psychological profiling of the amateur kind then, some forty years ago. Shock treatments were still all the rage, weren't they?

All in all though, when I was eventually stationed back in Sydney, I began enjoying the life I had at Bondi in my unit, along with travelling to see Anne in Melbourne and the inland trips to her hometown of Dimboola.

Yet some time later it dawned on me that I was becoming less interested in many things including a full commitment to my girl for reasons beyond me now, and then, so I began to wander in and out of relationships at home. I believe something inside me died after the incident at sea and my confinement to a military prison, even if my tenure was not as brutal as would be expected in a place like that. I believe if it had been I would not have survived mentally or physically. I was still a skinny little blond kid, and ripe pickings, I'm sure.

JRs Ahoy!

Ready for action

A ROYAL GUARD OF JUNIOR RECRUITS

QUEEN'S BIRTHDAY HONOURS

Her Majesty the Queen has been graciously pleased to approve the following awards:

K.B.E.
Vice Admiral V. A. Smith.

C.B.E.
Surgeon Rear Admiral R. M. Carless

G-G's VISIT TO THE WEST

The Governor-General, Sir Paul Hasluck, inspects a Royal Guard of Honour comprising of Junior Recruits from HMAS LEEUWIN after his arrival at Perth Airport on June 10. It was Sir Paul's first visit to his home State since his Investiture as Governor-General on April 30. The 96 Junior Recruits, from Collins and Walton Divisions, were members of the 24th intake of JR's who had their Passing Out the same morning. The Officer of the Guard was LCDR Johnson; 2OG was LEUT. McNally; Marshall was CPOQMG Plunder, and other Guard of Honour personel consisted of POQMG's Meyer and Logan, POCK Evans and POWM Bevan. The Band, under LEUT Clark, RANR, comprised of RANR and selected JRT Drum and buglers.

Pomp and Ceremony

GROWING IN IMPORTANCE

Opened as a Junior Recruit Training Establishment in July, 1960, HMAS LEEUWIN is today one of the major training organisations in the RAN.

Its growth since the first intake on April 7, 1965, has been steady and the recruits are passed on for further professional training confident of their future.

Training in the various divisions helps develop discipline, trustworthiness, initiative, courage and endurance and no recruit who enters LEEUWIN leaves dissatisfied. He studies and works hard, and he also has, in his recrea-

tion and leave time, sporting opportunities which allow him an opportunity to match himself in many fields.

Keenness is obvious and LEEUWIN's reputation in WA sport is now well established.

In recent months the establishment's face has changed considerably as teaching and "living" amenities have been enlarged.

The old viewpoints in these photographs may be familiar

to ex-LEEUWIN recruits (1 1963) but the backgroun won't be.

The four-inch gun mounti on the parade ground fa the new combined gall cafes, recreation room and Sailors' Club, all of whi were nearing completion wh these pictures were taken.

Up on the hill we see, place of the pre-war "she the accommodation blocks.

The other picture shows t new school block, includi the science laboratory.

Under the gun

MILK SHAKES, too, are in demand and here Chaplain Chetwynd, RANR, serves this thirsty lot of JR's (from right to left), DYKSTRA, GLASSON, BAIN and McCOLL.

State or Federal aid, and it relies entirely on local resources for its upkeep.

Its task is simply, to care for the visiting seafarer during his brief stay in port.

And so there is a chapel dedicated to St. Andrew, who himself was a man of the sea.

There is a shop, a restaurant where caviar and oysters may be had, or just a cup of tea, depending on one's tastes, and of course, a licensed bar.

There is accommodation available and each room has its own shower and wash basin with breakfast served in bed.

Television, table tennis, billiards, dances (three nights a week) and many shopping facilities are available.

The club is extensively used by J.R's from HMAS LEEUWIN (to say nothing of "Scruffie," and during the visit of HMAS OTWAY the whole crew was accommodated and victualled during the submarine's stay in port.

During the first nine months of this year over 75,000 seafarers made use of the club which is never closed.

SPINNING DITS OVER A JUG from left to right are LSUC Hamilton, LSUC Mills, and ABRP Hemingway.

Milkshakes all round Padre

Navy News asks you to support those generous people who help keep this paper alive.
You can't go wrong.

NAVY NEWS, November 22, 1968

Beating the hell out of one another

My rusty nail, the Vung Tau Ferry

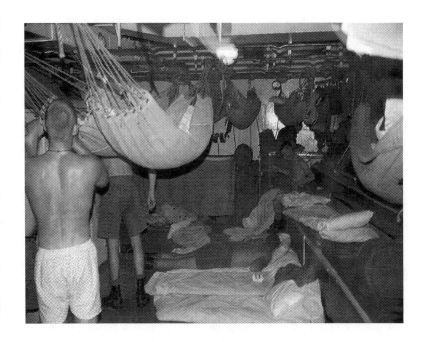

Pongos sleeping over

Gunplay on the Vung Tau Ferry

H.M.A.S. Stalwart and a jesting moment

Tragedy at sea.

A few years prior to this disaster H.M.A.S. Melbourne accidentally sunk H.M.A.S. Voyager with the loss of many lives including young recruits who were trapped in the engine room. A survivor described how an old chief clung to his sobbing wards and sang to them until he and the recruits drowned in the flooding compartment.

Darwin aftermath

HMAS ARROW pictured in Sydney Harbour before leaving for Darwin.

ARROW was carried out by Clearance Diving Team One, under the command of LEUT Dave Ramsden.

HOW IT WAS DONE . .

CDT 1 succeeded in clearing HMAS ARROW from under Stokes Hill Wharf on Monday, January 13.

Large pontoons were attached to ARROW at low water. As the tide rose, ARROW was simultaneously lifted by the pontoons and dragged clear of the wharf by tugs.

Two previous attempts to move the Patrol Boat failed when the lifting wires parted.

However, the third time was successful and ARROW was towed underwater to shallow water at Frances Bay, about half a mile from the wharf, where a detailed inspection of the damage was carried out.

Rear Admiral D. C. Wells, the Officer-in-charge of the Naval Task Group in Darwin, sent the following message to the Clearance Diving Team: "The recovery of ARROW in difficult conditions reflects great credit on all concerned. Well done".

FLEET'S WITHDRAWAL FROM DARWIN — PAGE 3

H.M.A.S. Arrow
before and after

Old boys and me to leeward

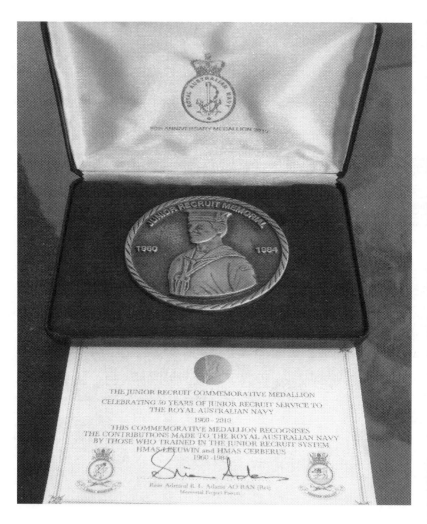

J.R. Memorial Medallion.

4ᵗʰ *Chapter*

A WEDDING

'One fool at least in every married couple.'

Henry Fielding
(Amelia)

Why am I including this marriage into a chapter of its own?

It's not so much the fact my getting married is so much entertainment value here, but it does stand on its own in regard to my confusion within the big picture. That is, to me the country and the ocean reflect a very different view of my interpretation of life, and to which was I to give my soul? Where did I belong and more importantly whom did I belong with? Nobody is my guess: at least not until much later in life.

I was raised in a semi-rural area where there was plenty of space to breath, play, live and love, with our home meandering down onto a crystal clear fresh water creek: so clear in fact you could drink its purifying water. We swam, frolicked and behaved much the same as others before us in this virgin land where our view of the world was luminous and unimpeded.

We were raised in a multicultural environment where, as I said at the beginning of my story, some nationalities had been killing one another on the battlefields a generation prior, and now we all lived in peace. We children travelled dirt roads on pushbikes in the icy cold of winter and the crackling heat of summer to attend to our recreational activities and schools, with only the occasional unarmed bully to interrupt our otherwise tranquil existence.

And yet the new country life I came to know with Anne at Dimboola was real, honest-to-goodness Australian country with generations of quiet, harmless and gentle folk with all their redeeming qualities who grace these outback towns.

I loved the pubs with all their photos and trappings decorating walls from a bygone era. A place where you could sit at the bar, have a yarn to a barkeep and upon finishing your beer you would lay your glass down to announce you had had your fill. A tradition still observed to this day in the outback.

My attraction to Anne initially was the fact she was different to all the other girls I had met because of her gregarious country qualities. And when this relationship eventually led me to meeting her family, I then fell in love with the idea of being in love with these country towns and with her people.

Her dad was a war veteran, as were many of the men from these areas who had absconded to the rural life to forget the horrors of war, to live a hard-working, yet casual life away from any trauma that seems to lend itself to the big cities. He had fought in the jungles where he described to me, only once, the horrors of war while we were drinking beer at the local pub, along with Anne's brother and some of his mates. Her brother had also gone to the city to work in a bank and regularly came home with his sister, allowing both to drive and to keep each other company, since the journey was considerable in time and distance.

Anne's dad had fought in New Guinea, as did my grandfather who volunteered for service in 1940 when he was forty years old and sent to North Africa. My pop was one of the last 'Rats' to leave the small garrison town of Tobruk on the edge of the Libyan Desert, then sent in to relieve the young 'chocolate soldiers' of the militia in New Guinea, so named due to the misconception they would melt in the heat of battle. The hardened Australian Infantry Forces stood side by side with these young men against the Japanese onslaught on the Kokoda Track where they eventually pushed them back with the loss of too many young lives against a battle savvy enemy. Moreover, grandad had previously served in the merchant navy as a deck hand during World War One.

He too had spoken to me only once in all the years I knew him regarding the war and it's repercussions on the human body and soul. He smoked three packets of cigarettes a day for his nerves until he died at age seventy-five.

He once told me of an incident his older brother encountered in World War One while on a battlefield in France after a massacre of allied and enemy troops, where, against the flames of burning debris and landscape, he could see the souls of the dead troops raising above the field of battle into the fog of night.

Grandfather was a great man who had left his three little girls in the care of his sister, Mary, because his wife, my grandmother, had run off with an Islander and his brother in the nineteen thirties. My guess he didn't care about his own welfare and his sister was more than capable of caring for my mother and her sisters; however, this is another story for another time.

Stories of hand to hand combat on the Kokoda where the will to survive was the hand on the throat of an enemy soldier who had surprised them, and the strength, through fear and adrenalin, to tear this enemy's throat out completely: my future father-in-law lamented as he laid his glass down.

Many stories from our country cousins who served were forthcoming, especially when enjoying a beer or two at the local(s). Most smoked and drank excessively, yet somehow managed to soldier on with the support of their families and communities. Many died before their time in their efforts to forget.

Lest *we* forget.

I was familiar with weapons by now and as a result I assimilated quite well for a young bloke from outside their realm. My knowledge with firearms secured me a position in their hunting trips, which were many and varied over a period of time. I had recently armed myself with a decent double-barrelled twelve-gauge shotgun, a twenty-two automatic and a 303.25 calibre bolt-action rifle for bigger game.

We hunted duck, quail, rabbit and hare, and we took our toll on some native species that were devouring areas of vegetation. We fished the lakes (now refilled after many years of persistent and hostile droughts) and used the hare meat to catch potato sacks of yabbies. These tasty little morsels resembled mini lobsters the same size as our large prawns, yet had a muddy taste to them if not prepared correctly. A large drum filled with fresh water, a bottle of vinegar and a bag of salt did the trick. The poor buggers screamed when they went into the boiling caldron causing them to disgorge and expel other impurities. Once cooked there wasn't a better tasting feed to be found anywhere, especially while sitting under a huge willow down by the river on a smouldering hot summer day, having a few cold ones, or around a back yard in the cool of the evening among the dried burning cows pats used to drive off the mozzies.

Winters in Dimboola where we sat around open fires, or a wood fired stove at midnight when we finally arrived after hours of driving, to find Anne's mum preparing us country eggs, bacon and fresh home cooked bread straight from the oven, with lashings of homemade butter. We sometimes watched the brittle and brilliant dawn of a new day after we had rallied for the remainder of the evening with full bellies, drinking, laughing and longing for a better world.

We hunted for our food and ate what we killed after it was prepared in the country way, as only country folk can. Now we find a world of scepticism as to the old ways and our colourful past, but then this was our parochial way, wasn't it?

English springer spaniel dogs accompanied us on duck and quail hunts with their mighty jaws able to penetrate skin and bone if need be; nevertheless they delicately returned dead and wounded prey undamaged by their sharp teeth. It was left to us to humanely break the neck of wounded birds, if the need prevailed.

These intrepid animals were virtuous and brave, obedient and loyal, as was the situation when my future father-in-law raised his shotgun to shoot, simultaneously the dogs were trained to drop to the ground on their bellies. This time though his dog dropped onto a deadly brown snake. It had known the snake was there, his master didn't. He died there where he lay, loyal to his last breath.

~~~~~~~~~~~~~~~~~~~

Prior to the wedding I had been transferred back to Sydney to the Patrol Boat Base at H.M.A.S. Waterhen and was piloting a diesel workboat around the harbour picking up and dropping off sailors and officers at various wharfs and bases. This was my boat and I captained it, so my word was law and all who sailed upon her understood this was my ship: such an awakening for me to be in this position while still a teenager.

I lived off base at the unit in Bondi, therefore had time and opportunity to wander around the inner city that was Paddington, with its cobbled narrow streets and terraces' standing side by side among the rich bouquet of jasmine, lavender and frangipanis. This was the area of my parents' birth where they had lived in the inner eastern suburbs as youngsters. We would come and stay with my Aunt Mary in the holidays with the beaches and the city only a short distance by tram, and while there was very little money to squander most were content with their lot in life.

I loved this area because it bought back so many childhood memories. Once I had become lost in the all so simular back streets after my First Communion, and kindly people safeguarded me until the police arrived; then made door-to-door inquiries until they located my frantic parents and relatives.

The area now had a smattering of old pubs and wine bars that had sprung up recently, and this is where I met a young girl who introduced herself as Joanne. She happened to be a nurse-in-training at the Royal Women's Hospital around the corner, and this little wine bar was her getaway, along with a few young doctors and other staff who made our hospitals so efficient at the time.

I had wandered in alone to reacquaint myself with the area I had grown to love as a child, and quite close by stood the façade of the home units for the popular television series Number 96 that was to be used innumerably during its five year run.

Joanne was a little blond thing; attractive in an odd sort of way with an elfish demeanour, yet when she spoke I found I was drawn to the mischievous smile, not only on her pretty face, but also in her voice. She had come down from the country (my ears pricked up) and had a little flatette around the corner she had rented by herself. Joanne and I hit it off and when she introduced me to her friends, including a young English doctor, I found myself welcomed into their world without hesitation.

Over the weeks I became intimate with her and friendly with this doctor with whom I had confided regarding my somewhat tormented standing in the world. I told him I was engaged to a girl from interstate and that I wasn't sure if I was doing the correct thing in bringing her into my world here, away from her familiar life and loving family.

He advised me of many things and gave me a phone number of a friend with whom he suggested I discuss my problems.

The intimacy with Joanne began almost immediately with my going back to her place after a few too many drinks only to discover on the first night she had bled during sex; I was shocked:

"What's this Joanne?"

"This was my first time Mark."

"What," it wasn't a question.

"I wanted to give my virginity to you."

I couldn't think of anything constructive to say, so all I said to her was:

"I didn't really want it. I'm engaged to a girl in Melbourne and I was only looking for some company with maybe something else if the opportunity came along."

"Oh," was her reply.

"Look, I don't really know how all this will pan out, but I'm really interested in you and enjoy the company of your friends, especially Doctor John, so let's let it ride for a while, and we can still see each other if you want."

"Yes, I'd like that." She then asked, "Why do you like John?"

"He's helping me through some issues I have with life and the navy and a few other things I'm not happy about."

"Like your engagement?"

"I'm torn is all," I said.

"Do you love her?"

"Yes, I think I do, and yet it could be the fact I'm in love with the idea of being in love with a beautiful person from a beautiful family, and coming from the country, the same as you. I really love the bush and its people."

"You could love me too, you know."

"Yes, I could mate, but I hardly know you, whereas I do know Anne."

With that the relationship and the company of her friends continued for some time, although it came to a head on a weekend when Anne surprised me with a visit while I was having a conversation with Joanne in my flat. The only other person there was my cousin who I have mentioned had been six months behind me in recruit school.

Joanne had come to tell me she was pregnant, but before I could get my head around the situation there was a knock at the door.

'Who in the bloody hell is that?' I thought at this important moment, discovering my potential invitation into fatherhood.

And there was Anne with her overnight bag, looking radiant. I introduced her to Joanne and told her she was a friend who had dropped by for coffee, still she could tell by my fumbling and helping Joanne on her way that we were more than just friends.

When I took Jo downstairs I told her we would talk about it after the weekend, although my heart was still with Anne at that time.

When I returned to my flat Anne didn't talk about it at all, and never again was it mentioned, which somehow puzzled me. I can only assume she thought as long as I chose her then any indiscretions would be ok, especially being away from each other for long periods. This was country comfort for you.

Anne left after three terrific days to return to Melbourne and at the first opportunity I went around to Jo's flat to have a talk to her but she wasn't there, and when I inquired she was not at work either.

Weeks later with still no sign of her I did finally happen upon her friends and the good Doctor John at their wine bar. They told me she had left to return home, and nothing else. John was sympathetic while I cried into my wine about what a fuck-up I was, and he agreed. He said I was young but still had time to reorganise my life and come out of my dark hole. He suggested I call off the wedding so as not to draw an innocent into my world at this particular time. It was too late by then.

I wonder to this day if Joanne had her child and if I have a progeny running around somewhere who would be close to forty years old today. Or was it a ploy to gain my undivided attention? I can't be sure owing to my uncertainty as to her emotional credibility at the time, since mine may have been hazy enough for both of us.

Then there was Kay, a most beautiful divorcee ten years older than myself, and dying of cancer.

I mention Kay here because when I married Anne, Kay would come and visit me occasionally, so I consider her to be a part of this story, with a twist.

After Jo I was still in a place where I was considering my future and how to manoeuvre my way around the situation I had found myself in with Anne. It's not as though I didn't love her; I'm sure I did at the time. It was the idea of being able to escape from my present world, if only temporarily, to another place in my head if she were there beside me.

I had met Kay at the now familiar wine bar where she was sitting alone reading a book, then with a few drinks under my belt I approached her and said:

"Hi, I'm Mark, and you are truly a good lookin' woman. What's your name?"

"Kay, and how corny was that comment?"

"I agree," I said. "Still, you are attractive so thought I would come over and tell you. Are you waiting for someone?"

"No."

"Then can I buy you a drink?"

"No, I'm on medication."

"You ok though?" I asked.

"No, I'm not."

"Can I sit with you?" I said.

"Why?"

"Because I want to."

"Ok," she said. "Why not."

We talked for hours until the bar closed, and strolling arm in arm to her flat a short distance away we chatted on like old friends.

We talked again until three in the morning, over a bottle of wine: she had decided to have a drink when she was home, and then confided in me she had cervical cancer. Her husband of only a year had returned to the west when he found he couldn't accept her condition and then wouldn't come near her.

Initially she had chemotherapy, followed by a full hysterectomy leaving her with nothing of her womanhood, except the fact that at twenty-eight she was the most gorgeous and graceful lady I had ever had the pleasure of meeting.

We kept company until I set off to get married. We had grown so close I couldn't bring myself to tell her of my betrayal, although by this she had only a short time left owing to her terminal illness, which was now out of control to the extent her mother had come to Sydney to take her back to the family's country home. Once again, my love for our country cousins had overwhelmed me. My only keepsake was a photograph of her, taken a few years prior, holding her pet cat; nevertheless, this photo is a work of art I assure you, and I have it still to this day. There's something about her natural long blond hair tumbling around her shoulders and her soulful rich, deep blue eyes. Something I find difficult to decipher, even to this day.

She died by the time I had returned with Anne to set up home in my unit at North Bondi, and this is where the twist in this brief tale became a catalyst in my belief in the hereafter. Not as though I didn't believe prior to this, since I had come to the conclusion that forces were at work somewhere, somehow. As I have said previously, I had time to contemplate my life while my employer held me in custody at the will of Her Majesty.

We had been married only for a very short time, and occasionally while asleep I could feel a presence hovering over our bed. While I didn't think it had a malevolent intent, this presence would float down over me and smother me with, I think, love. I physically had to catch my breath and push it away so I could sit up and gulp air. I knew it was Kay.

This continued on and off for some time until I told Anne about Kay and her influence on me prior to our marriage. She again took it in her stride and told me to grab her hand and squeeze it when this presence embraced me again and then she would wake me.

It happened a few more times, yet with Anne's help and comfort these apparitions began to fade. I was never frightened and went willingly to bed and sleep every night. I guess it was a message to be honest with others, and with myself, conveyed to me by Kay with love, and I refuse to believe there was anything sinister in her intentions. A very real connection existed even if there was a world and some years separating us.

Those advocates and sceptics alike who debate the pros and cons of 'sleep paralysis' take note: many things are explained away all too easily, yet some things remain very real to those who have actually experienced them.

While I'm on the subject of the supernatural I will tell you of an incident that ensued, again, not long after Anne and I were married and Kay was still making her presence felt.

We had planned to visit Anne's parents in the not too distant future so I said to her:

"Hey Annie, I really need to trade my shotgun in on a new Remington automatic so I can keep up with all the other hunters down home. They're leaving me for dead where kills are concerned; six shots are more effective than two. What do you think?"

"Good idea," she said in her always-obliging way.

So off I went to the very local gun shop/arms dealer to have a chat to the owner who I had come to know reasonably well. A few minutes later I was standing at the door, gun in hand to trade and about to enter, when I felt a cold rush of air hit me.

It was too quiet, with no sound at all and after taking just one step in I said:

"Hello, Bill, you there?" Not a breath, nothing.

Then I found myself out on the pathway again, still with my gun in hand, and how I got there I can't recall to this day.

I actually felt myself to see if I was dreaming, or had I passed over to another world for that matter. I left there and returned home a couple of hours later after having finished some other shopping.

Anne said to me as soon as I got in the door:

"Where have you been? I've been worried sick."

"Why, what's up?"

"Bill up at the gun shop has been murdered, and someone else too."

"You're kidding, I was there a couple of hours ago and no one was there I think, because I called out."

"They found them dead, executed they said, behind the counter."

"Fuck me," was all I could muster. Then I told her the story of what had happen to me when I was there and that I felt, not so much afraid as tentative, although it was quickly forgotten in the ensuing hours with the idea I would go back later to trade my weapon.

Something pushed me out of the shop in a cold rejection of death on this hot summer day, I know. The killer was still there behind the counter, crouching down over his victims like the vulture he was, waiting for me to enter further.

"I'll wait until I get my shit together before I go to the cops. I just need to figure it all out first. Tomorrow maybe," I said to Anne.

The breaking news the following day saw this fat, miserable nobody who had confessed and was now in police custody, so I didn't do anything about it.

I haven't retold this story until now.

~~~~~~~~~~~~~~~~~~~

Dimboola. You may have heard of this play? And still performed to this day, about a country wedding where the audience are the guests, and witnesses, to the proceedings surrounding the nuptials of a young couple from different religious denominations, their roots similar, but their relatives' worlds apart.

The audience are treated to all the hilarity of drunken guests, belligerent parents, cantankerous relatives, fights, a whacked out priest and a bridal table you wouldn't wish upon anybody.

This play, dedicated to a country wedding, was derived from two or three comparable weddings at the time out of Dimboola, and a little township not far away called Jeparit (the birthplace of our famous Prime Minister of yesteryear, Robert Menzies), and was written by Jack Hibberd at the time we married. His actual part in the major stage production was his portrayal of the local newspaper editor.

My side of the family and friends came from near and far to our wedding, still talked about to this day. They included my folks, sister, cousin, uncle and aunt, friends from schools and shipmates, with all their partners at the time.

My best man, Joe, had to be held up by his wife during the ceremony because he was still smashed after our buck's night the evening before. He had driven from Queensland and had only just arrived fifteen hours prior to the service at the local Catholic Church. During the reception he passed out at the bridal table and couldn't be revived, as a result another shipmate, Steve, stood in. He did a terrific job even if he couldn't remember the bride's name.

The reception at the local pub was rowdy and a great success and continued until sunrise with guests wandering around the streets at dawn looking for their partners, cars, rooms or homes. Since we were staying at the local motel for the night we were witness to the antics of the zombies as they hobbled, vomited, fell over and generally made happy nuisances of themselves, only to start again after a hearty country breakfast supplied by local wives and Anne's mum.

I should clarify here not all the cacophonic situations in the play were attributed to our wedding, although some were similar reproductions of incidents that had occurred.

Twice we were among the guests/audience when we went to see the play in Sydney not long after and were welcomed with open arms when we disclosed our origins in regard to the ceremony itself. We had also invited friends to come along and see for themselves what a country wedding was all about. They all agreed the play was a hit and wished they had been there with us, and would have only for the fact they weren't invited. We had the whole town at the service as it was, and half the town at the reception. After the ceremony we had wandered down to the hotel and were obliged with drinks at the bar where we had congregated until the function room was ready. Such is the country connection within its ranks where the locals all knew each other with their kids growing up together.

On a more sombre note, Steve, my stand-in best man and my friend, broke his back in a motorcycle accident on his way to visit his parents not long after the wedding, along the same route by way of Dimboola to Adelaide. He just so happened to be a passenger on his own bike that night: the rider, uninjured.

~~~~~~~~~~~~~~~~~~~

Unfortunately the marriage didn't last, yet the memories do linger still to this day.

For those who wish me ill will let me tell you that on the first evening I deserted her I was involved in a horrific accident when my new Volkswagen Beetle was literally torn in half by a drunk truckie on a lonely miserable sodden stretch of road in the early hours of my new lonely miserable life. I was driving to my parents home some one hundred miles north of my recent abode when I was rammed from behind while pulling over to the side of the road, due to poor visibility. As the rain came down so did my guard and there I was again released from another nightmare, this time by the local Rescue Squad, without a scratch.

Later I tried to alleviate my guilt for the predicament I had put her in by seeking a church dispensation and annulment. It was granted after much ado, but this didn't ease the burden of ruining her life. She went on to remarry an impostor who claimed he was a Vietnam veteran and couldn't stand the sight of rice, jungle, Asians and the like. She divorced him when she discovered in a conversation with this idiot's mother that he hadn't been to war at all, let alone served his country in any capacity whatsoever. She never had children.

The irony of my life continued with my future and present partner, Lisa, living around the corner from us in this, out famous beautiful beach area. And while not a country lass at this time, she was soon to spend a generation as a Tamworth girl when her adoptive parents spirited her away to the country life after they sold their business. Furthermore, my father had played football for the Eastern Suburbs team along with Lisa's adoptive father in the forties. Lisa was five, I was nineteen and my school friends were still having their beds made for them at home.

A short while after my escape from the marital home saw me needing to associate with women who had disabilities. I guess I needed to be needed. Over a couple of years I dated a deaf/mute girl, an amputee, a drug addled young mother whose child had recently died, and a disabled young woman who was bound to life in a wheelchair: all victims of life's callousness.

I saw this as a type of welcomed penance because I had deserted Kay in her time of need, only to damage another good soul in Anne.

My hypocrisy had no bounds, still, at the time I found it necessary to help as best I could. It may be noted no one was hurt by my good intentions, I'm sure. Nevertheless, I think now my involvement may have been misconstrued as a new beginning for one or two, in that they may have considered their options rather limited due to their infirmities, but I never believed that. I saw in them what many other potential partners would eventually see: beauty, strength and determination.

I would eventually gain entry into university to study social sciences, such was my resolve to finally try and help others. Until then I was doing a shitty job, I'm certain.

5th Chapter

PATROL BOATS

'The essence of life is statistical improbability on
a colossal scale.'

Richard Dawkins
(The Blind Watchmaker)

I was finally given a permanent posting to the patrol boat and minesweeper base on Sydney Harbour, H.M.A.S. Waterhen, where my harbour boat duties continued, including going to sea on a regular basis to trial the new Attack Class patrol boats; definitely my calling to be left to my own devices as an engineer, much the same as Steve McQueen. Not so though, in that there was always someone to answer to, therefore with a crew of only nineteen all of us had to pitch in to see the vessels operated smoothly.

Powered by twin sixteen cylinder Paxman diesels with a top speed of 24 knots or about 44 km/h these little barques had a displacement of around 150 tons fully loaded within her 100 foot (32 metre) hull.

One Bofors cannon mounted on the bow, two .50 calibre machine guns and an assortment of other small arms, all maintained by the crew, as was the remainder of the vessel, even to the extent where I was relegated to cook once in a while.

We hauled stores and ammunition aboard constantly to some of the twenty boats that were to be commissioned in the time I was still to serve; nonetheless it was a satisfying period, since these commands were more relaxed due to the intimacy of all who sailed on them. Not the intimacy you may be thinking, such was the scandal on the H.M.A.S. Swan at the time when a group of sailors were transferred and/or discharged due to their antics with each other's tackle. Unfairly, it became known as the H.M.A.S. Fluffy Duck.

This was a different navy altogether; more relaxed, albeit the whole system worked better than I had been accustomed to on other ships. We sea-trialled a few of these boats including the Assail, the Advance and the Arrow, the latter sunk in the Darwin hurricane disaster of 1974, with the loss of naval personnel.

I was still married, although I felt more relaxed with the crew including officers, a chief and two petty officers, along with other ratings such as myself, than I did at home with Anne. So I volunteered to go out on all sea-going trials, including the delivery of the Assail to Darwin after a crewmember and acquaintance had killed himself in a motorcycle accident.

A most disturbing incident, I can assure you, when I had to identify him late one evening, owing to my being on duty at the time the police informed us his remains were now in the city morgue. At this particular time I was the only one available who could positively identify him, therefore I was sent out in a navy vehicle on this storm-ridden night and drove to the inner city a few miles across our iconic bridge to see to this unpleasant task.

My date with the Reaper was a most disagreeable experience, especially for the fact that the lad had been decapitated, although the considerate gatekeeper on duty had placed his head on his torso. His tragic death an accident on a wet night, as so happens in too many instances.

His minder, a coroner's assistant and keeper of the dead, was a good bloke and we became friends post-navy, until he overdosed on alcohol and medication due to his macabre existence: an appointment he secured at the same morgue *after* he had to identify his deceased wife and young child who were involved in a tragic motor vehicle accident a few years prior to his own demise. This is a story for another day though.

My memory of the incident now is as surreal as in a dream, along with my friendship with the gatekeeper whom I met on a number of occasions late in the evening, at not only a very local bar a minute's walk to the morgue, but also in the morgue's own lounge area, outfitted like a comfortable small inner city flatette. We would drink and talk about life and death until a new victim was delivered into his safe hands.

Prior to this we set out on the Arrow to see if all was fair-sailing with her, so she could eventually protect the waters off Darwin along with the Assail and the Attack, especially from Indonesian poachers who were a constant problem fishing within our borders: a situation we were to confront in the not too distant future.

We sailed out of the harbour in the Arrow on the most spectacular spring morning I can remember from those particular exercises. We were exuberant, such was the weather, and the calm sea shone like a sapphire in the morning light. We dropped anchor some distance off shore and proceeded to launch an attack on our sea creature friends in the form of testing all the weaponry on board. We threw cans, barrels, plastic containers and the like overboard only to then give this beautiful ocean a touch of lead poisoning: an insensitive exercise to say the least then, and now, in our polluted world.

With .50 calibre machine guns mounted, including a wealth of other deadly weapons, we let fly with whatever firearm was available to us. A few dead fish bobbed up to the surface and then an albatross came over to investigate the furore. Although this beautiful bird was drifting high it was easily visible to the naked eye, when unexpectedly our machine gunner decided in all of his not-so-infinite wisdom to take a few shots at it. We saw feathers fly as it came down and hit the water dead, only a few metres from the boat. We all stood dumbfounded. No matter if your own life depended on it you were not to harm these wondrous creatures. After all, the albatross was the sailors' friend.

The skipper came charging down with a look of such apoplectic rage you would have thought he was going to have an aneurism on the spot. He then grabbed the rating responsible for this gross act of stupidity and kicked his arse repeatedly, until the freak wave hit us.

Out of nowhere on this clear, calm and beautiful morning we were hit amidships by a wave sent by the gods to punish us for this sacrilegious, abominable and malignant act. Stores, weapons and personnel went over the side as the boat lurched ninety degrees, with the ones who remained below decks hurled around like peas in a tin can. Some sustained minor injuries and had to be returned to base shortly after we regained our composure. I had hung on for grim death as I saw the monster approach, at the same time yelling out some inconsequential nonsense to the others. Some heard my warning cry, too late though.

The albatross had launched itself, with the help of Neptune no doubt, onto our boat and there it sat perched until a brave older petty officer gently pitched it over the side after we had all refused to go near it.

We hobbled back to shore with no real damage to the small ship, yet our feathers were ruffled, so to speak, as were the captain's and his having to fill out all sorts of forms to explain away the happening without detailing the assault on his subordinate. No one else would support the offending sailor either; it wasn't an issue in the final evaluation of events.

As I have written, this fine little craft, the Arrow, saw its own death a few years after with the loss of sailors during Darwin's obliteration. A ship tortured by a prior incident whose short-lived life was fraught with mishaps and breakdowns, I'm told.

Such are the tales of the sea from sailors down through the ages, all true, I assure you.

And what of the sailor and his misjudgement in his successful attempt to draw down the wrath of the sea gods? He went down with his ship.

It was during this period at Waterhen that I had stints on a wooden hulled minesweeper moored at the base, the H.M.A.S. Snipe, and always the joke when serving on one of these oldies that the men were made of steel and the ships made of wood, unlike the rest serving on steel hulled vessels.

The minesweeper was somewhat larger than a patrol boat with its ability not to attract magnetic mines, of which there were still some floating around off our coast, due to extensive mine laying during World War Two by both the Japanese and German navies, along with our own mine layers. When the ones that evaded our retrieval eventually eroded their shackles they would float about for years, and at this time, forty years ago, there were sightings at sea including some washed ashore in remote areas. It was then up to the navy to see to their demise.

I also had the not so pleasurable experience assessing my future on an Oberon class submarine.

Our submarines at the time were diesel powered tin cans with supposedly two crews to man them due to their extensive deployment to seagoing duties. When they arrived back home the crew would be replaced with another crew to repeat the drudgery over and over again.

I ventured onto one of these fish to have a look at the possibility of joining up for underwater sea operations with a promise of more money. An underwater allowance as if to confirm it was a payment for serving in a dangerous and closeted environment where you shared your *fart-sack* (bed or bunk) with other sailors while you were on your watch and they were not.

The trouble was they couldn't secure a full two crews together for each of the vessels, even though you would have had a holiday in England for a few months for ongoing training prior to spending the rest of your life underwater.

In the end some poor seafarers were out for months due to the shortage of crews. My cousin served on this class of submarine and has never been the same since. Not insane at all, he just needs the air and space around him with solid ground under his feet.

He told me of a conversation he had with the young skipper of his sub when serving during special operations in unfriendly waters. The captain said if they were intercepted by the enemy and an attempt was made to board her, he was to shoot himself with his handgun so generously provided after he scuttled the submarine with all on board, who would also happily to go down with the ship.

"Bullshit," says I.

"No bullshit," says he.

He asked the captain to drop him off at the next port.

Besides, I couldn't abide with pommy officers for a start, let alone being underwater for months on end, and in confidence I was advised of this by a friendly chief from my base who had served on them for a period. This same chief confirmed he had heard the crews for these tin cans were still at a nominal level owing to fewer volunteers coming forward: bad news travels quickly in the service.

The subs were also experiencing difficulties in their performance and were constantly being serviced for malfunctions. 'Fucking great, Davy Jones locker awaits,' I thought.

Patrol boats were the only option for me.

Because of the close proximity between the officers and crew on these plucky boats I had the pleasure of meeting some weird and wonderful characters like 'tripod', a petty officer who stood six feet tall with a weapon a good eleven inches long. He would hang his towel on it in the morning and wander off to have his *dhoby* (shower) with his toothbrush slipped conveniently through a hole in his circumcised foreskin. This is a feature I am discussing in detail because, apart from his audacious mettle, he had a tattoo of a snake spiralling around his penis with the head of the reptile sitting on his knob. A true work of art, unlike the tattoos we all raced to disfigure ourselves with at sixteen or seventeen. There were W and Ws' tattooed on arse cheeks signifying WOW when the recipient bent over; service identity numbers, blood groups, tits, vaginas, Popeyes', little devils shovelling burning coals up into bum holes, tattoos of ugly women with the inscribed dedication, 'The sweetest girl I have ever kissed was my mother'. You name it, I've unfortunately seen it due to the close proximity in our living conditions.

Anyway, this sailor once boasted to have carried three wet towels, and his toothbrush, of course, on his manhood to the bathroom. A feat I never had the privilege to witness, although it wouldn't have surprised me in the least.

He was married to a WRAN (Woman's' Royal Australian Navy) petty officer, who stood not five foot nothing and would have blown away in the slightest wind, such was her frame along with her demeanour. He would tell her to be waiting on the dock with a mattress tied to her back so he could *clear tubes after she had assumed the position.* This was the terminology used to assert his male bravado by saying she should get down on all fours while he takes her from behind and delivers his goods into her. We thought him a gentleman that he considered her welfare and comfort by demanding she strap a mattress to herself: funny though, his little spinner always looked happy, yet somewhat pale and gaunt after he had had his way with her upon returning from sea-going duties.

Over the next couple of years we serviced, repaired, maintained and generally ironed out the bugs, of which there were many. Some under warranty from the builders, some minor, some major, although *all* of these little ships had to be soundproofed, since the noise from the diesels was deafening, especially if you came off watch while at sea and needed to bunk down.

We fished from Jervis Bay in the south and north to Newcastle while piloting these boats, a distance of some 300 nautical miles, about 350 miles or 600 kilometres. Some rough seas prevailed, but mostly my time on these jaunts were enjoyable, so much so, as I have said, I volunteered to take the Assail to Darwin after the unfortunate demise of my fellow engineer.

We sailed out of Sydney on a grey, bleak morning and the drizzle had dampened our spirits to such a degree that all was quiet among the crew, yet the smell of the diesels and the drone of its engines warmed us: warmed me, anyway. We were to be away for some time and I suppose we were going to miss our families, wives and lovers who weren't going to be there to comfort us. I felt the same, strangely enough, since I had volunteered to take this voyage. At the same time we were all excited because the size of the craft and the distance we had to travel was out of context to other voyages on what could only be described as floating cities.

I had once spoken to a black American sailor and he disclosed the fact they had military police patrolling their ships' corridors and alleyways, thanks to the possibility of being mugged for the personal belongings you may have been carrying around at the time. Mugged on your own ship? Fucking yanks. Was this the beginning of the end for this once proud liberator of the world? It seemed a little thing at the time and something you would laugh over. Now I'm not so sure.

It warmed as we motored north and we all pitched in to cook, clean, navigate, along with other wheelhouse duties, engine room tasks, gunnery exercises and emergency drills.

I was relegated to cook for a few days considering all was well in the engine room with the chief and his petty officer making sure our boat was motoring along smoothly. Not that they didn't trust their *stoker* (me), however, there were still issues with some of the machinery. When all was running how it should have I was then sent in to maintain the power plant.

My cooking skills were limited though, but then my enthusiasm was abundant, so I used my imagination, like all good chefs, and concocted numerous delicacies to tantalise the taste buds of my crewmembers.

Eggs scrambled with butter, milk, cheese, onion, tomato, garlic, tinned ham, and a touch of chilli, paprika or curry. Baked beans a-la-Bru with the same ingredients as the eggs minus the milk and butter, all went down well for breakfast with tinned ham sandwiches for lunch, which I teased with an assortment of flavours and spices. Although most of our stores came in tins and packets, apart from hardy vegetables, frozen meat and the fresh fish we caught along the way, some valiant storemen had infiltrated our goods with small containers of spices from who knew where at the time. As a result, along with my other culinary delights, my fish dish was something for which I became renowned, using again my ability to whip things up quickly. This served me well in later life when I had established my own food haunt.

Whole fish in foil on a bed of lemons, liberally buttered, peppered or spiced, shallots/onions, stuffed with garlic: easy, tasty and healthy. I know today this seems common and simple but forty years ago you could call it imaginative.

As we moved further past the Tropic of Capricorn things were warming up and the seas at dawn and sunset were the most spectacular works of art I would ever see. The imagery of reflections dancing on a calm sea stunned the most hardened of us, with the skipper stopping the boat and shutting down its engines so as to deafen us with silence and blind us with its beauty. At this dawning moment with most on deck and those below coming up top to see why we had shut down, only to be also dazzled by Mother Nature's breathless dominance. Simultaneously we all were aware of our insignificant presence in her world.

Suddenly, immediately before us, the dead calm sea erupted into what only could be described as a bubble bath of activity with schools of fish dancing around on God's fingertips while dolphins had their fill, as did we when we gathered ourselves into a fishing party to reap His creatures for our menu.

We moved further north to Cairns along the Great Barrier Reef where the dolphins led us along a van Gogh palette of fish and coral while we swam and fished for delicious cod until we had to move on under the umbrella of naval time restrictions.

We docked in Cairns when one of our generators decided it wasn't going to start after a minor service, and as a result we had ten days to play in this beautiful unspoiled paradise until the appropriate parts arrived.

While I was on watch one night, and the rest of the crew had ventured into town, I was left on my own to keep safe our boat. Because we were tied up along with other voluptuous, beautiful and expensive boats and yachts I had let my mind wander off to another world of wealth and fineness, until activity roused me from my inner journey.

I was unaware of how king the king tides were in this part of the world until I was on the verge of hanging our boat out to dry, however, with the help of a few kindly folk we managed to let out the lines.

The following day someone had dobbed me in, but the skipper didn't see any real harm this time through my lack of attention, and as I explained to him, I had shit myself and it definitely wouldn't happen again. He stopped my leave for two days and that was all right by me.

One morning I was first up, being the cook of the day, so I decided to have a wander on shore to see if I could scrounge up some exotic titbits to liven up the meals, when out stepped a young blond woman of about seventeen or eighteen from a magnificent yacht moored nearby. She was wearing nothing but a sheer white sarong that happened to blow open in the early morning breeze when she walked up the few steps to land immediately at my feet, so to speak. No one on her boat, and us alone, and in an instant of pure insanity we fell back into the bed of this emancipated girl; then it was over, sooner rather than later. She kissed me and we parted ways with me forgetting about my previous mission and returning to my ship. No names, just a few words telling me her rich older lover was away for a few days.

Our journey continued north and the weather remained calm. Then on a clear moonless star-filled sky not far from the northern most point of our journey and while I was at the helm with a petty officer of the watch, we hit a metal object, or what sounded like a metal object: a thump and scraping sound along our hull.

I said to the duty petty officer:

"What the fuck was that?"

"I dunno, you hit it."

We stopped the boat and all the crew, including the captain, now aroused from their sleep, came on deck to see what had happened.

The skipper busted into the bridge and said to me:

"What the hell was that you hit Bruhwiller?"

"Buggered if I know sir. It's pitch black out there and it had no navigation lights to speak of."

"Let's go back to see what it was, don't you think?"

"Could it have been an old mine, do you think?" I said to him.

"Fucking hope not," said the duty officer.

"Skipper, if it was an old mine don't you think it would be a bit silly to go hunting for it in the dark, after all we beat it once, we may not be as lucky next time if we hit it?" I ventured.

"Maybe sailor, but it's our duty to see to these things, isn't it? So let's get all the spot lights fired up and go mine hunting."

It must be remembered an old submerged mine in the black waters of night is not an easy target to locate even with spot lights, still we turned around and after getting geared up and armed to shoot it out of the water if we had to, we commenced the hunt, only to be relieved and disappointed at the same time not to be able to locate the bloody thing.

We anchored until daybreak and still couldn't locate anything that resembled a metal object floating anywhere around us, then we re-reported the situation to command who sent an aircraft to search for the mysterious phantom.

I was told I might have sunk it, since it seemed the only likely scenario. I thought to myself, 'not only had I been spared again but maybe I had spared others by sending it to its grave.' This was only an assumption, yet with my attitude lately of at long last doing something worthwhile for my fellow human beings, it seemed a fitting outcome at the time.

During World War Two both the Allies and Axis powers laid mines in Australia and New Guinean waters with our own navy laying thousands of mines both in open waters and around our main ports.

After the war we were responsible for clearing them from our territorial waters as part of an international minesweeping effort, hence our navy was assigned the task of sweeping Australian waters. Based in Cairns the operations began in 1946 with over a thousand personnel involved in a sweep that was considered extremely dangerous, and with the loss of H.M.A.S. Warrnambool with some of her crew when it hit one of our *own* mines, those dangers were certainly confirmed.

Obviously at the time I was on patrol a few of the mean bastards were still around.

~~~~~~~~~~~~~~~~~~

As we rounded Cape York we encountered a fishing boat some distance off and after making contact we cruised on over to have a look see, when much to our surprise and pleasure two young tanned women presented themselves on their deck wearing nothing but the most negligible of briefs and waving to us. These disentangled modern girls were a breath of fresh air to us back then, as they were to all young men. They were part of the new age travellers at the time, working their way around Australia for a few dollars and their keep.

The small crew wanted fresh water and beer in exchange for the most succulent seafood found in the area. The girls also requested a hot shower, and when the captain obliged they came aboard as they were, as friendly as can be. The skipper then led them below and didn't emerge until a half hour later with them both: the privilege of the higher echelons of humanity. Who says power corrupts?

I prepared much of the fruits-of-the-sea with the help of their experienced crew, who knew of such things, then we sat down on deck to eat with our beer ration(s) on only what can be described as a day in paradise and we all agreed that this was better than sex.

Or was it due to the bromide generously pervaded into our powdered tucker, the same potassium bromide used copiously if at sea for lengthy periods, which saw us with limp dicks and hardly a hard-on in sight? Or was the use of this substance an urban legend? We had discussed this at length in our time, yet came up with no definitive answer except for the fact that sexual arousal seemed to be at a minimum while at sea for lengthy periods.

Our next stop was Thursday Island, off the tip of our most northern headland, and a somewhat primitive port in the day. Because there was some type of civil unrest we were ordered to stay on board and arm ourselves while standing alternate guard duties.

Apparently some whites had moored their pleasure craft at the local wharf and had planted themselves in the local lean-to pub; drunk themselves into oblivion, then offended the village head and his daughter, only to then suffer at the hands of the natives for their misdeeds by having profuse damage done to their persons by way of the machete.

While these poor souls had been removed from this paradise lost it was our job to restore calm to this volatile situation. A call to us only a day prior led us into this port where we now found ourselves, and we were to stay for however long it took to settle matters through international or Australian parley.

It didn't take long: the first night we stood guard over our floodlit ship with more lights directed toward the entrance to the wharf from where we could possibly be attacked. And there a gathering of listless barbarians-at-the-gates armed with the customary machete or two flashing in our spotlights and waving a menacing not-so-welcome barrage of abuse toward us.

The skipper ordered the .50 calibre machinegun to be mounted on the foredeck in full light and when all went quiet he ordered our gunner to cock it. Have you heard a heavy machinegun being cocked in the still of night? This formidable sound had an intimidating effect thus causing the natives to disperse every which way on the double. The bleeding heart may not appreciate this politically incorrect approach, yet were we not intimidated?

Anyway, no more problems, with a diplomatic solution agreed upon soon after.

Into the Gulf of Carpentaria where we encountered more of our own fishing boats and since we were always warmly welcomed we often traded with these stalwarts of the sea. Both men and women who told us of their adventures and battles with illegal fishermen, cyclones and other experiences in the north of this vast country; how they survived during the mean seasons of the wet and wild summers; the dangers of the ocean with its many deadly sea creatures; the struggles of making ends meet, and moreover how they persevered throughout, as was the Australian way.

My time in the north was to be short-lived, albeit the most rewarding of my service. Darwin itself could only best be described as a large country town primarily made up of prefabricated dwellings, which were soon to be knocked over like matchsticks by the wrath of Cyclone Tracy.

This multicultural and diverse population from all walks of life including hippies, Australian and foreign backpackers, natives, travellers and the like, drinking beer, vodka tonic, rum and coke all in stubby holders, without which your drink would virtually melt before your eyes. Us and this spirited melting pot of humanity would watch the most spectacular sunsets we had ever witnessed in this paradise of ours, where you could sit on the wharf behind the open bar feeding large Barramundi by hand with stale bread and scraps from the bistro.

Off again from Darwin around to Broome from the Arafura Sea into the Timor Sea where we finally confronted our northern neighbours poaching our sea life. One of the many tasks required from the patrol boat fleet was to repel these buggers from illegally fishing our waters; still they managed to annoy us with their persistency.

Dawn, a few days out, we found a rather dilapidated fishing boat with a crew of six skinny foreigners, and as part of the boarding party armed with our trusty SLR automatics two of our team then began dumping their catch overboard. As I was standing at the stern of their boat one made a sudden move as if to stop this disposal of our sea creatures. I lifted my rifle ever so slightly and said:

"Hey!"

And maybe would have let go of all my emotions and frustrations from the last six years in one short burst, when the captain called to me:

"Stand down, sailor."

I didn't, until he said again:

"Stand down, now and come back on deck. The rest of you come back too."

After we boarded our boat the chief told the fishermen to leave immediately, nevertheless they began back-chatting us:

"Tinggalkan kami sendirian anjing!"

A petty officer standing on the bow stepped up to the .50 calibre and said to them in a clear menacing voice while cocking the weapon:

"We won't be leavin' you alone while you fuckin' well keep coming into our waters, and *we* are *not* dogs, so fuck off now or I'll kill you all where you stand and no one will be the wiser. Fuck off now!"

A cold stare from our skipper towards his charge for his undiplomatic approach was interrupted when the fishing boat quickly turned around and disappeared into the blue.

"Not appropriate behaviour petty officer."

"No sir."

"Don't let it happen again without my say so."

"No sir, yes sir."

The skipper then said:

"Good work though and nice interpreting. They will probably complain to whoever when they get back to wherever they came from."

"Don't think so sir. I've done this before and they know they were in the wrong. Can be nasty bastards if you let 'em, that's for sure."

"They understood you well enough," said the captain.

"Sure they do. They know our lingo for sure."

"As for you Bruhwiller, killing illegal fishermen is not quite what the navy is about at the moment, ok?" said the skipper.

"No sir. Thought he might be going for a weapon is all."

"And what would you have done?"

"Shit first sir, then fired." I said.

With that he ordered a burst of fire away from the intruder just to let them know we were armed and dangerous. We asked if we could lend a hand by expending some ammunition and contaminating the sea as we had done on numerous occasions previously. So we armed ourselves with an extra assortment of weapons after the captain agreed to our request, and then we let rip. I believe he considered this the best remedy for venting what had become an edgy situation: good officer and an astute skipper who knew his stuff, no doubt.

I'm sure to this day the illegal fishing boat disappeared more abruptly than would be expected, maybe with a message to their compatriots to keep away from this area too.

As for me, would I have fired in anger? I really don't know, however, it's funny how when put in a hostile situation, self-preservation takes precedent over common sense. And most importantly, it depends on the state of mind of the individual at that particular moment. Doesn't it?

Finally we disembarked at Broome, our final destination before heading back to Darwin. We were keen to observe the locals, since this settlement was coming into its own after its earlier beginnings as a ramshackled costal village built many years prior, chiefly to support the pearl industry.

Shortly after one of my buddies left the wharf and stepped into the shallow water he yelped:

"What the fuck did I just step on? Fuck me dead." Then he went down like a bag of spuds kicked over in a storeroom.

I yelled to him:

"What's the matter with you?"

"Fuck, I just stepped on something and it hurts like a bitch."

Two of us raced over to him as he laid on his back sobbing in pain, and when we had a look at the underside of his foot we saw the dreaded spike from our friendly stonefish species protruding from the instep of his right foot.

There was only a few of us around at this time considering the rest of the crew had already left on a Broome adventure, so we half carried, half lifted him back on board and laid him down on the bench cushions surrounding our dining table. We then proceeded to pump him full of scotch that we had stashed away for the voyage. We also poured it over his swollen foot and began to slice it open with a razor blade to get to his malicious adversary. This was not routine obviously, but it was the only thing we could think of to relief his pain at the time. It actually frightened the hell out us to see someone we knew and liked screaming in agony. Then half pissed, he drunkenly screamed at us:

"You fuckin' bastards are all cunts and I'm gonna kill youse when I get up. I'm gonna fuckin' well fuck youse right up, shoot the lot of ya....."

I had my turn in getting it out and as he finally faded it suddenly released its grip. We left it on the table to show the crew, then proceeded to wrap the foot and leg firmly and comfortably after dowsing it with lots more scotch.

By this time Bill had passed out completely from shock and alcohol. All was forgiven though when at last he came back to the land of the living.

We did a good job, so said our superiors, although a little unconventional and due to our quick response we had our mate up and about in a couple of days. Our cutting job and his hangover were serious issues, yet both mended quickly.

We arrived back in Darwin a few weeks before Christmas 1974 and went about a normal daily routine, except the weather would melt your resolve with fans running day and night to relieve you from the stifling, oppressive humidity of the northern summer.

It was almost impossible to get drunk owing to the profuse amounts of sweat pouring out of you the more you indulged. Also, there were more than enough suicides among the thirty odd thousand population due to their inability to cope with this brutal, draining climate. Even though the afternoon thunderstorms brought some relief it would only be a matter of minutes, not hours, before the humidity took over once again. The roads would dry just as quickly after the rain ceased.

I was offered the opportunity to stay on as a permanent crewmember, but declined due to my situation back home with Anne waiting for me. She was somewhat alone in Sydney away from her home state and as a result my conscience had since reached out to me.

I considered my time would come now I had experience on patrol boats and I was sure another vacancy would present itself in the future.

I was to be billeted at H.M.A.S. Watson situated at the head of Sydney harbour in a resort style base for those passing through to who-knows-where, and for those about to be discharged. Just a dream draught where I could be reassigned to patrol boats at any given time, with absolutely no pressure, no bullying, no real regimentation, but still a tightly run, clean and well organised base for a smaller detachment of sailors and officers.

I said to Anne shortly after my transfer to this base:

"Why in the hell couldn't the navy have been like this all the time?"

"Why don't you stay in then?" the always-obliging Anne replied.

"I just may do that."

I flew out of Darwin on what only could be described as a 'redeye' flight twenty-four hours before Cyclone Tracy hit and devastated the tropical township. While I wasn't fussed on boarding a twin prop to fly to Katherine, Adelaide, Melbourne, then onto Sydney, it did allow me to get home on Christmas Day. Consequently I went for it armed with a bellyful of grog and two half-gallon Darwin beer stubbies, one of which I still have to this day, unopened. The other I smashed falling up steps trying to catch my flight.

6ᵗʰ Chapter

CHRISTMAS 1974

'Man is born to live, not to prepare for life'

Boris Pasternak
(Doctor Zhivago)

I arrived back in Sydney early Christmas morning in a state of disrepair owing to the long, tedious flight. Being somewhat hung over, with no real news filtering through from our distant north, coupled with an ethnic, hard-to-communicate-with taxi driver, I was delivered safe and sound to my Bondi unit.

Anne came rushing to the door as I fumbled for a key and opened it at the same time, then wrapping her arms around me she said:

"I've been so worried about you."

"Why?"

"Darwin's been wiped out by a cyclone."

"What?" I said, having heard her yet not quite understanding the enormity of the statement.

"Darwin's been blown off the map by a huge cyclone."

"You're joking. I was just there."

"I know, I thought you hadn't got the flight and you were still there. Lots of people are missing and everything has been blown to bits."

"Shit," I said. "I better report to the base to see what's going on." Even though they wouldn't have had a clue as to where the hell I would have been at this time.

"You should get some sleep first because no one really knows what's going on there. Communications are cut as well," said Anne.

We kept the radio and television on while we had a Christmas breakfast, then I slept for the rest of the day.

When I awoke I phoned my new base and asked if they wanted me in asap.

My orders were to report the next day seeing they were still organising ships to leave immediately after they were loaded with food, water and medical supplies, pre-fabricated dwellings, tents, beds and personnel.

When I arrived early the following morning there was confusion as to where I was going to be deployed. They were aware I had just returned before the bastard storm hit, thus were reluctant to send me off again, in that they considered I may be too effected by the scenes I would encounter, especially if my crewmates were injured, missing or killed. They had adopted a wait and see approach.

There was also the slight dilemma with my ongoing status, since the navy had recently and generously allowed us junior recruits an option to give eighteen month notice to leave the navy if we had served at least four and a half years, giving a total of six years' service to your country.

I had put in my notice of discharge eighteen months previously so I could start a new life on the outside while still only in my early twenties. I had served five years before giving notice to leave because I considered my life on patrol boats to be more fulfilling and this had delayed my decision a few months. Notwithstanding, my marriage, my imprisonment, my unpleasant beginnings as a Junior Recruit continuing on the Sydney and Stalwart, all weighted heavily as to my state of mind, although with the promise of a promotion in the near future I then took an initiative with my commander telling him if I was to be promoted immediately I would withdraw my resignation. This decision would have meant re-enlisting for an additional three years. I would have had to wait eighteen months before I could tender my resignation again, then be discharged eighteen months later. I guess I really wanted to go back to Darwin and stay given the fact they needed me there. They needed us all there, especially those who knew the area.

As fate would have it the newly elected government, in all of its wisdom, began to dismantle the armed forces after our withdrawal from Vietnam in 1972 and as a consequence promotions were at a minimum. I really needed no more than a gentle knock back to gratefully head in my own direction to begin again.

Some of my buddies went to Darwin on the flotilla of relief ships and finally, when they had returned, told me their stories and the stories of those who survived. I also had conversations with a few civilians who had been billeted at my base after being flown out of the devastation. Our southern bases had taken in survivors for resettlement, since the poor souls had no other relatives other than those who were living in Darwin. Resettlement had become a priority with these naval bases to be their temporary home.

There had been no refrigeration for days before the troops arrived in the disaster zone; therefore people were buried in mass graves to avoid disease, owing to the bodies having bloated within hours. Mass evacuations by air had been ongoing leaving only around ten thousand people behind to volunteer their services and help reorganise and rebuild. The overwhelming conditions and lack of fresh water meant the work was slow and tedious for months on end, with badly decomposed bodies found under the rubble previously undetected, or impossible to retrieve, until heavy equipment was bought in. Their remains, and those of the servicemen killed, if not buried there, were housed in ships refrigeration until proper arrangements and identification was confirmed.

As the transient population of the area was never determined and records or census never kept, likewise with the seagoing folk, both legal and illegal, a true indication as to actual loss of life will never be revealed. Some put it into the hundreds without including our own Aboriginals. However, it was a consensus of opinion among the old timers who stayed behind that the natives had gone *walkabout* at the onset of the torrid conditions. After all, they had been here for thousands of years, therefore it would stand to reason they would have left the area due to previous ancient lore regarding adverse conditions, which no doubt had been handed down from their ancestors.

As told to our troops, some of the native elders had warned the locals with whom they had come into contact, that a major weather event was imminent. Unfortunately, and to an extent, they weren't taken seriously. They would be nowadays.

Some old diggers also told of their nightmare days when the Japs were attacking them some two generations prior and how there were many more casualties than reported, such was the case now due to rapid burials because of the heat and humidity, the isolation of some communities, illness and contamination.

The Aboriginal elders and old locals told of the Japanese that had actually landed on our shores in a remote area during the bombing campaign, and over on Christmas Island as well, only as a reconnaissance exercise and very few in number. Their intention was never to invade us at that particular time, albeit only to keep us in our place by fear and intimidation. After all, our armed forces personnel and other allies stationed there were only a token presence earlier during the war within a population of scarcely three thousand. Actually, I had heard this very same story when I was stationed there only a couple of months prior.

I was having a beer with a mate, Peter, in our wet canteen and who had recently returned from Darwin to also complete his service here at Watson. He had served his full six-year stint, which was his full deployment due to his having joined as a 'regular' recruit at eighteen. He had been shipped off to Darwin on the H.M.A.S. Melbourne to do his duty and the first thing he was ordered to carry out was the tracking down of looters, worst still, armed looters.

He, having the rank of a leading hand gunner, along with a company of nine other armed servicemen, set off to capture these villains and if necessary shoot them down like the dogs they were, and to bury them where they were felled.

"It never occurred to me that I would have to do that cause I went there to help out, not kill some prick," he said.

"And?"

"There are some real desperates up there and being so isolated and having such a large population of deadbeats wandering about who-knows-where, I guess there was bound to be a problem."

He continued:

"The place was a stinking hot shithole with nothing left standing. Fuckin' roofing iron and small yachts and boats flung up into trees and shit. I was told the government sponsored the building of the place and didn't bother to provide enough funds to build the shacks properly in a cyclone prone area, so they all just blew to fuckin' pieces."

I told him I loved the place in all of its simplicity, although it seemed everyone, then and now, loves it in the dry season, but when the wet hits it's unbearable. I was beginning to feel the heat myself by the time I left, that's for sure.

He went on to tell tales of hope and despair and I could see it affected him, especially when he told me the story of a couple of looters they encountered out in the demolished suburbs.

"What the fuck are you cunts doin' there?" He told me his leader yelled to two of these armed bandits.

"Drop those fuckin' guns and get over here, now."

"When one took off the leader let loose with a burst of automatic fire over him; this stopped him dead in his tracks. The other froze still holding a weapon," said Pete, and continued accounting for the leader's unique colloquialisms.

"If you don't drop that peashooter now I will kill you where you stand, you cunt."

"The gun dropped to the ground and both were told in no uncertain terms to get over to us," Peter said, and went on:

"When these two got over to us we discovered the one he called a cunt was one."

"Was one what?" I asked.

"A cunt, a scruffy young bird."

"Shit hey!" was all I could say.

"I'll tell you now, I was shit scared for them because I thought he was going to shoot them on the spot. Instead he said he was going to hang them there, and marched them over to the remains of a tree that was still partly standing. I nearly pissed myself then and there cause I know he meant it, this mad fuckin' chief in charge," said Pete.

"The only thing that stopped me was the bloke who he was going to hang pissed himself first."

"What about the bird?" I chipped in.

"She was pretty cool, hey, but they both cried and pleaded for their lives, the poor bastards."

"So, what the fuck happened?"

"Oh, he shot 'em both."

"Bullshit," I volunteered.

"Yeah, bullshit. And we buried them there under the tree."

"Bullshit," I said again.

"Yeah, bullshit," he said. "Fuckers deserved it though. We fucked 'em right up."

I still don't know to this day if he was fair dinkum or just dramatising the fact they beat the shit out of both of them and took them back to Camp Tracy, as it became known during reconstruction.

Rebuilding took three years and this time they were constructed of brick and steel, unlike the house of sticks the big bad wolf had blown down.

Peter now lives in Darwin in the dry season and travels in his caravan back to the southern states for the summer.

It never ceases to amaze me the resilience of the human spirit when it seems to take over common sense and drag you back to a place you once thought was the arse end of the earth.

Ask those who fought in any war why they return to visit and/or live in a land they once saw themselves and their comrades suffer, get injured and possibly die for.

~~~~~~~~~~~~~~~~~~~

From some survivors' recital, records and from Peter's account:

Early morning Christmas Day the cyclone destroyed Darwin with winds of two hundred miles per hour killing more than seventy plus (an unofficial number only). Within a short period the navy embarked on our largest peacetime relief effort with some thirteen ships, a dozen aircraft and a few thousand personnel. Only some three hundred sailors were stationed there at the time of the disaster.

Of the four Attack Class patrol boats moored there at the time, the Arrow was sunk with the death of two sailors, the Attack was beached, the Advance and my boat, the Assail, were damaged along with the destruction of the naval base itself; the communications station was also extensively damaged.

Search and rescue was limited due to the extent of the destruction to both civilian and military communication networks and as a result many people were left to their own devises, such is the case when communities are plunged back into primitive survival; hence, pillaging and looting were rife among some survivors.

The first foreign ship though arrived as early as the 26th of December with Red Cross workers and blood supply relief, followed by H.M.A.S. Balikpapan, Betano, Flinders, Melbourne, Brisbane, Stuart, Hobart, Stalwart, Supply, Vendatta, Brunei, Tarakan, Wewak and the submarine Odin.

Our pussers were responsible for clearing and securing over four thousand houses in the suburbs, and with many survivors left with nothing and sent south to our land bases, the place was fast becoming a ghost town.

Included in the clean-up was the assessing of the Arrow, which was then scrapped. The Assail and Attack were both towed and eventually recommissioned after extensive repairs.

From his and other accounts they cleared land, re-roofed homes and buildings, cleaned up schools and many other facilities. Foodstuff and other abundant rotting garbage from homes, stores and warehouses had to be gathered and disposed of quickly, since they were becoming a health hazard to all. Cars and trucks were made serviceable again, as were air-conditioning units, refrigeration and other electrical equipment required to sustain the living.

By the middle of 1975 the minesweepers/minehunters Ibis, Curlew and Snipe, were used to locate sunken fishing boats and other hazards located in and around Darwin harbour.

~~~~~~~~~~~~~~~~~~~

Again, sitting in the wet canteen at H.M.A.S. Watson soon after my enlightening conversations with Peter and others, I had a discussion with a bloke I had met only some months prior; a good hearted fellow, separated with kids, broke and living on the base.

"Buy us a beer will you Bru?"

"Buy you own fuckin' beer Jimbo."

"Skint mate. I'll fix you up payday."

"We only got paid a few days back."

"Skint mate," he said again.

"Ok Jim, but what's the go with your dough?"

"Pokies, can't get past 'em. Fucking cost me everything. Missus, home, kids, rels, mates, everything," he confessed.

"Who have you seen about it, anyone here?" I asked.

He told me he didn't want to confine in the navy because it would be on his record, just as pissheads and druggies hid their addiction to alcohol and drug use, and oddly enough there seemed to be a few here on this base. What we now consider mild drug use was then considered a very real undesirable affliction, much the same as homosexuality.

Times certainly change.

Was it just coincidence or was I becoming more observant and receptive to my fellow man?

"Look Jimbo, I know a bloke through a doctor mate I met a while back at this wine bar in Paddo. Why don't you have a word with him to see if you can beat it?" I wasn't going to tell him he was a shrink. Pessimism and head doctors went hand in hand back then and still do to a certain extent, I'm sure. I was more open-minded though.

"Gee Bru, do you think that will help?"

"Fuck knows, but it's worth a try, don't you think?" I said.

Over the next few months, until my discharge, I seemed to be directing others to seek outside help for their problems. This since my mate had experienced some satisfaction and passed the word around. And although my head may have been in the wrong place still, I was able to cope with life outside the service, to an extent.

These poor bastards were at a loss when it came to dealing with the pressures of life on the outside, considering everything was laid on for them in the service with beds, meals, television, leisure activities, budget grog and cigarettes being fully provided. It didn't really matter what went on in the outside would, provided you presented yourself for duty you were considered to be fit and productive.

I guess that's all it came down to really.

The problem with real-world actuality, when it came to many junior recruits leaving the service, was an attitude of not being able to cope with being spoken down to, yelled at, bullied and generally kicked around, such being the case with myself, and my cousin. We, like many others, were to eventually work for ourselves, and while not the employers' dog to be kicked, we were to be quite disciplined in the livelihood of our own choosing. It was a case of giving in one hand and taking from the other in regard to our naval breeding: regimentation versus rebellion.

Let me again emphasise not all junior recruits would have been subjected to the myriad of trials and tribulations that many of us had surrendered to. I can only guess this was a matter of good luck and/or good fortune, insofar as the branch of service they entered just may have been more nurturing in their approach to their junior sailors. Could it be said those who chose to seek a branch *above* decks didn't capitulate as readily as those who worked *below*? Again this may be a generalisation, so don't go jumping up and down if you were a J.R. and disagree. It's also worth a consideration if the first ship or base a junior recruit was drafted to, after his release from naval training, happened to have a softer approach toward his youth and inexperience: lending a proactive hand instead of an inactive one, if you like.

〰〰〰〰〰〰〰〰〰〰

In 1975, after my discharge, the first film I saw at our city cinema was 'Papillon', where Steve McQueen's character finally escapes from the French penal colony of Devil's Island.

Melodramatic, I know..........

Let me now show you an email I received via my intake's official website, however, I will not disclose the identity of the sender and will only let you see a portion of his correspondence referring to the 2010 Commemorative Reunion:

I have been really tossing and turning about the upcoming reunion in July and have procrastinated about renewing my passport to get back across the ditch - DVA recently sent me my TPI card too and aside from an expired passport and with the exception of my birth certificate I have nothing here in NZ that identifies me as an Aussie so I was pleased receive my DVA card. I know that I will not be attending the reunion - this may sound silly but please no offence is intended whatsoever: I don't think it would be very good for me to 'go back' because deep down in my heart of hearts this would not be a good thing for me to do - clinically it would not be useful to revisit the past and this was indicative as recently as 2008 when one of our intake visited me here in Wellington and as a result I'd 'come unstuck' emotionally immediately after the visit and that was a good indicator to me to avoid 'going back'.

I hope you all understand and accept my apologies in not attending JRTE this July.

Best Regards

> DVA.....Department of Veterans Affairs.
> TPI......Totally and Permanently Incapacitated.
> NZ......New Zealand.
> JRTE....Junior Recruit Training Establishment.

A SAILOR'S EPILOGUE

'What is life? It is the flash of the firefly in the night. It is the breath of a buffalo in the winter time; it is the little shadow which runs across the grass and loses itself in the sunset.'

Crowfoot
(Last words)

Life went on with no regard for its consequences, as loves came and went, opportunities along with friends came and went and relatives passed.

In 1975, after I had left the navy, I took to working for Whitlam's *Labor government, since he had pulled the plug on his armed forces and had frozen promotions, spending and recruitment, instead spending billions on his own agenda of creating a government controlled enterprise called Australia.

I'm sure to this day, married or not, I was settling into navy life with a promotion on the horizon and a career on patrol boats; however, this time the government intervened with the forces being plundered and pillaged to the extent we wouldn't have been able to defend ourselves against a troop of radical boy scouts.

To give you an example of government waste at the time, I applied for a government bus-driving job just to tie me over, thanks to having completed a heavy and light transport course while serving.

I was collected in a chauffeur driven car and delivered to Sydney's airport, then flown to Canberra where a driver conveyed me to a government building for my interview.

From there I told the driver to take me around the city for a look-see, since he was at my disposal for the duration of my visit, and then to wait for me while I had lunch at a hotel before my flight back to Sydney. Again to be chauffeured from the airport to my home after a hard day at the office: all this for a bus-driving job, which I didn't get anyway.

I had been a Labor supporter, as were most of our parents, and their parents before them, yet this government at the time, much the same as any serving government, I surmise, thrive on waste and ineffectual policies presented to us by ineffectual politicians who have never turned a sod of earth in their lives. Nepotism in politics and in other intrinsic internal departments festers like a carbuncle in the joints of this nation now, and I fear, the once 'lucky country' is now referred to as 'the not so lucky country'.

"What's with the politics?" I hear you say.

At my age I'll shout from the rooftops:

"I'm allowed to protest."

I'm apolitical now, in that I think all politicians are tarred with the same brush. Are we over-governed? You bet we are.

Our fathers and their fathers before them fought and died for this country only to let it fall into the hands of political terrorists that milk everything from the system they possible can before retiring to their mansions and lovers with free lifetime travel and chauffeurs, while also accepting a whooping pension. All this and our ex-servicemen struggle by on non-indexed retirement funds continually seeing their hard earned and fought for pensions dwindle. And who has their pensions indexed?   Politicians.

I believe if you have served your country for twenty years or more in a dangerous field of operations whether it involves the armed forces, state and federal police, fire or rescue service, et cetera, you should be entitled to a pension paid to you *after* you serve out your time. Don't you?

Ask politicians if they have to wait until they are sixty-five for their pension after only a few years in their cushioned trenches.

Also, I bleed for the welfare of our children among our growing population of feral underclass. Teens paid to breed only to have their offspring dragged up and thrown unto the scrap-heap of society; immigrants and queue jumpers who only grow to hate us; society's acceptance of violence so profound and prolific that our young will never fully understand the true nature of violence and the waste it leaves behind in its wake; still they want to experience it, taste it, live it, devour it, and then have to pay for it for the rest of their lives, along with their victims.

Enough of my soap box spruiking...........

I went on to achieve my Higher School Certificate at TAFE and entered University, which was another adventure in itself insofar as my ongoing life education was concerned. I was introduced to opera and ballet by enrolling in a feminist course while studying philosophy, and why would I enrol in these courses? Maybe I needed to be enlightened. I remain friends with one of these successful ladies to this day.

She was also to witness my first parachute jump when we set out to thrown ourselves from a small Cessna the old fashioned way by clambering onto the strut of the wing while balancing on a narrow step and a wheel, of which the pilot had kindly applied the brake, then throwing ourselves off backward into the abyss hoping the static line would release the chute. My first jump ended with my parachute being tangled and ripping my helmet off as it released. My intrepid will back then was to calmly unravel the tangled chute lines and grab the toggles only to crash land with the wind behind me. I didn't have enough time to turn into the wind, but still managed to bend my knees and roll as instructed. No tandem jumps back then, just a quick instruction before you were flying free.

Everyone on the ground shit bricks, as did I when reality finally hit. They thought my head had come off initially and when realising it was my helmet they switched focus to what damage I sustained when I hit terra firma. I was ok and not a scratch to be found. I did sustained damage the following day after getting as drunk as a lord after the jump.

They never found the helmet. They were relieved my head was intact, along with the rest of my person when they finally got to me; my friend confirmed from the ground it was a frightening experience. I said it was from my position as well.

Once again: need I say it?

During this period I had met a young woman, Anne (whom I will refer to as Anne number '3' at this point) '3' off a rebound, and had two children to her. After four years she left and I raised my kids with the subsequent help of my present lady, Lisa, who still lives with me to this day in a typical country area with free-range and organic produce on hand, and not too far from the sea along a rather expansive undulating river. Eventually tearing myself away from both the country and the ocean, I now live between them, well away from any large city.

Prior to meeting the mother of my children I had been a state government bus driver, a cabbie and worked as a television extra to help pay my way through an uncompleted senior education.

Finally, I was a single father with a small business and struggling to make ends meet, although I did take on the responsibility for representing single dads as a government initiative to sort out the mess that was our welfare system. All voluntary, all encumbering and non-discriminatory, these initiatives, along with other edicts from concerned citizens, were eventually implemented, to a degree.

You could say I grew up quickly in these years with a lock-and-load attitude that I had never really believed I had prior to my single parenthood. It may have always been there lurking, I realised later. Furthermore, I conducted basic cooking classes for young mums and helped out others with their cars, lawn mowers, electrical and other problems they may have had that required a jack-of-all-trades type person.

And having had some recent practical experience working in a state rehabilitation centre, and with some TAFE/University knowledge, I gave advice to numerous people who sort it, but only with the recommendation that they should seek professional help from a number of free clinics, social workers and Chamber Magistrates available at the time. I had my days in court too, armed with free legal advice and no legal representation, to keep my children living with me.

To this day I make suggestions, not in the capacity of an advocate for returned servicemen, but as an ex-serviceman who has gone through the minefield that is the Appeals Tribunal, so that others may apply for compensation from the military.

I have also worked tirelessly for the 'Your Rights At Work' campaign a few years ago and was issued a commendation with a limited issue medallion. Ok, Ok. No big deal, yet it was a fight I was willing to undertake, since my four children were being treated like so much garbage in their respective work places, along with other persons I have known in similar situations.

Presently I have a social commentary website to promote fairness and wellbeing.

My sins have been prolific though. The most terrible sin of all is the squandering of life, then I began to turn my mortal soul around when I met this fine lady who took me from a dark place and showed me the light, even though my problems were still many and varied, with all my adversities eventually catching up to me. Age and excess will always find a way around your denials, won't they?

I have now written a couple of small books not only as a cathartic exercise, moreover to advise consumers and the general public of the many pitfalls to avoid when dealing with the obtuse miscreants who so dominate our lives.

You could say this narrative you are reading now is a prequel and final chapter to my non-fiction anthology.

I have also set myself a course writing short stories and some poetry, one of which I won a literary award you have read at the beginning of this book, although somewhat modified.

Please don't misjudge my intentions here in this tome. As Socrates wrote, *'the unexamined life is not worth living'*. Thus it is here with mine, and the many adventures of my youth.

Later, a love affair with a teenage girl, Anne '2', while I was at University as a mature age student, was both enlightening and deep, enduring for three years until I asked her to marry me. Alas, she had fallen in love with her lecturer at college, as they do, and ran off with him to our nation's capital to complete an honours degree. They didn't last, as they do, or don't do; still, she went on to marry, have children and is very happy.

After my divorce from Anne '1', and up to the period I fell love with Anne '2', prior to Anne '3' with whom I had the children, I lived the life of the single well-paid government employee in the little suburb of Lavender Bay where I had a spectacular view of the most beautiful harbour in the world, Sydney.

This one bedroom crib (as the kids call it today) was my home during my bachelor years in the seventies when love was free and left no lasting tell-tale signs on your body or psyche to speak of: innocuous sex would be the best description. Wives, girlfriends, lovers and fiancés were all available in this hedonistic and narcissistic, yet safe world, except when I was pursued by the jealous husband of a woman I was having sex with: he was a cop out for blood. As luck would have it he caught up with me in a very public place where I said to him I was unaware of their marital situation. We still had a few choice words regarding the fact that his wife may have been involved too, being one half of the offending couple, then his mate pulled him away amidst his lame threats, and that was the end of it.

The drugs were mild, although the insidious bastards around Bondi eventually led us into another dimension. And the chance of contracting a social disease was almost non-existent, although I did use the old navy 'after sex remedy' on occasion.

The odious eighties is another story with the pugnacious and greedy taking over; where entrepreneurship was king with most ending up earning a living on council road gangs; where HIV,

STDs, chlamydia and herpes were all the rage, and unfortunately still are. And leaders who eventually took us to war again, over oil this time.

My theory is greed has led us into global crises, in that it creates so much more poverty, and from poverty springs terrorism.

Do I now believe in a higher authority? I would be stupid to believe otherwise looking at the many incidents, accidents and mishaps I have dodged throughout my life, essentially a life fraught with near misses.

I do believe in Karma and *what goes around comes back around to you,* whether it be good or bad. Don't you?

I have paid for my past indiscretions when situations were reversed and caused me as much heartache as I had imposed on others.

I do believe my good Catholic parents prayed for me, with my war veteran grandfather's guidance and our family priest who gave me a gold Saint Christopher medal, the travellers saint, when I was fifteen prior to my setting off on my life's journey, and which I still wear to this day. Though somewhat scarred, I have survived due to their love and concern for me. The scars are merely life's war wounds and should be revered as the tell-tale signs of a life lived, with stories and advise to be handed down to those who don't understand such things, until they themselves have lived.

My parents and relatives who loved, cared and prayed for me are gone now, therefore it is up to me to watch over and pray for those who are left behind, while I still have breath.

I would like to stand one last *watch* though, to see them through a little further on their journey.

Laugh if you will at my finding my faith again, nevertheless, let me assure you, and you can take this as gospel, there are no atheists in the trenches.

'Tis a chequer-board of nights and days
Where destiny with men for pieces play;
Hither and thither moves, and mates, and slays,
And one by one back in the closet lays.

Edward Fitzgerald

The Rubaiyat of Omar Kahyyam

ANNOTATE

The following paper was presented to Dick Smith for the chance to win fifty thousand dollars in prize money by investigating the whereabouts of a billion dollars in wasted taxes on the navy's phantom purchase of antiquated Seasprite helicopters from the U.S.

No, I didn't win and didn't expect to. No one else did either, and I can tell you now there were some professional submissions from prolific watchdog investigators who write on these matters for their journals.

I think Dick donated the money to charity, although I see this as a cop-out by reason of some presentations did get right to the point and expose the misdealing. However, through Dick's eyes I consider *no one* was going to reach his expectations: the charity donation was a good compromise though.

My purpose was not to castigate the Royal Australian Navy as such; nevertheless it was an exercise into the frivolity of governments' mentality and the waste perpetrated upon us all while they continue to enjoy the fruits of *your* labour.

Enjoy:

A LAYMAN'S CONSIDERATION
OF THE SEASPRITE DEBACLE

The problem with the Seasprite was that one hand didn't know what the other hand was doing when it was decided an 'Offshore Patrol Vessel' was no longer on the agenda, insofar as the Malaysian/Australian co-venture was concerned.

We were to co-develop this ship as a coastal defence strategy, and its fleet air-arm was to include the specially remanufactured smaller chopper, the Seasprite, since it would have the ability to actually land on the O.P.V.

Incidentally, the Defence Department and the government at the time failed to connect the fact the smaller chopper was not suited to carry the special weaponry needed, and in use, by our own existing navy. And now that Malaysia reneged on building the new patrol boat we were left holding the bag. No boat, no need for the revamped chopper, and no comprehension from the powers above that one was to go hand in hand with the other. Simply put, and apart from the weapons system, the smaller reconditioned, made to fit Seasprite helicopter, was no longer required because the accommodating Offshore Patrol Vessel was now dead in the water, so to speak.

Add to this the contract handed to Kaman Industrial Technologies to manufacture and install sophisticated control systems into antiquated Vietnam era helicopters retrieved from mothballs, was doomed to failure from the beginning, especially since the contract had no fail-safe clause, ie: nil damage clause, nil insurance in the event of the unexpected or the unachievable: that is, no penalty clause the government could use to escape the confusion it found itself in.

The 'too-hard-for-Kaman' contract was then handed over to Litton (a major U.S. military manufacturer with affiliations to Kaman) who then reneged on its obligations to us by jumping onto another huge deal offered by a much larger U.S. company. No fail-safe penalty clause here to fall back on either.

Add again another factor to further complicate the tale: the then Keating Government was in bed with the Labor party's major donor Transfield (now Tenix) who was in bed with the Malaysians. So, once the Offshore Patrol Vessel was sunk along with the Seasprite chopper deal there were no happy campers, since Transfield was also a major player in defence contracts. As we move further on I will show their contractual connections to the government.

While it was a Keating government baby it should have been scrapped prior to the Coalition's win in 1996.

When John Howard was elected he became concerned with the cost of cancelling contracts to these, I'm sure, well intentioned, but not so bright companies; nevertheless, bright enough to have a watertight penalty clause stipulating if we cancelled, the penalty to the Australian taxpayer would have been substantial.

Even as late as March 2005 the Defence Department was still extolling the virtues of the Seasprite and its capabilities, therefore the whole episode lies with the Minister of Defence (and his advisers) in the Keating Government from around 1994-96 through to scraping the hopeless things by the present government some ten years on; however, most notably with the Howard years, where inevitably within a full decade some compromise agreeable to both parties could have been reached.

Are our military strategists in the pocket of the U.S. military machine buying up its old equipment with the hope of refitting them with the new ultra-modern aviation equipment required nowadays? And were they aware buying new choppers would have been equal in cost, if not cheaper, than the old/used machines/frames/skeletons they purchased? New Zealand and other countries managed a better deal by purchasing simular, albeit new U.S. helicopters.

Now for the events leading up to and including the previous Labor and Liberal mismanagement of this debacle (and other defence bungles coming to light):

Firstly, I must tell you of my sympathy for the Liberal Defence Minister who resigned from his portfolio in 2006, Robert Hill;

acknowledging the, 'challengers for his successor including grappling with an unwieldy department with serious accounting problems.'

His lack of knowledge when entering his portfolio in 1996 as to the joint venture of an OPV with Malaysia (who we were not on intimate terms since the Keating reference to Malaysia's head of state as a recalcitrant) while still honouring contracts and old debts owed to Transfield for their major contributions to the now opposition Labor Party. Plus Transfield's affiliations with the Malaysian tender had put him/us on a political sword's edge from the very beginning.

Secondly, add to this the fact Robert Ray, as Defence Minister for the Keating Government from 1990-1996 who was responsible for this *whiteboard method of doing business, plus his advisors' connections to Kaman (the innocent remain innocent until proven guilty), it's little wonder it was headed down a road to perdition.

Robert Ray's departure two months prior to his official date of retirement, just after the announcement of the cancellation of the Seasprite deal, is probably not worth mentioning. And the 1.3 billion dollar cost to the taxpayer, and then some (who has taken into consideration other penalties for our breach of contract?) is probably not worth mentioning here either. Is it? Or is it?

Hugh White, who I'm sure is innocent of any wrongdoing, is a Professor of Strategic Studies and a Fellow of the Lowy Institute, and was a senior official in the Department of Defence from 1995 to 2000 where he acted as Deputy Secretary for Strategy and Intelligence, and knowing the Defence Department is huge and inflexible in its attitude to our sticking our noses into their business, certainly someone, somewhere, among these elite advisers were aware of their department's policies and expenditure: or not, apparently!

Which leads now to Mr Peter Jennings, who I'm sure is innocent of any wrongdoing, and his advisory status and affiliation with the Massachusetts Institute of Technology, of which he is a Fellow, who has an affiliation with Kaman, that has offices close to the M.I.T., which has an affiliation with our Government and the Lowy Institute through the American Australian Association, which in turn have affiliations with everybody imaginable.

Mr Jennings was the 1ˢᵗ Assistant Secretary for Co-ordination and Public Affairs for our Defence Department; nevertheless, he was defence adviser and then Chief of Staff to the Minister of Defence from 1996 to 1998, with likewise other important responsibilities. He is a Fulbright Fellow at the M.I.T. where he wrote of Australia/U.S. relations.

Now to Mr Howard's Minister of Defence Ian McLachlan from 1996, who implemented the government's Defence Reform Program cutting key personnel from important defence positions and relocating many of them to combat operations, and in so doing may have left important decisions in the hands of sub-administration personnel.

Again, I have said, it beggars belief other such brilliant minds behind such ill-informed politicians were not aware of any major financial defence-spending strategies embraced by their employer, the government.

My only reasoning is for our own ongoing safety in the region we occupy, is/was to safeguard bilateral agreements by the 'yes sir, no sir' attitude to our master, the U.S.of A. That is to pay 'protection money' so our enemies are kept at arm's length. Furthermore, taking into consideration whichever political party takes power it has no intrinsic control of the defence department's manipulation of their own budget; therefore, when it comes to their own defence agenda they answer to none other. One must also consider U.S. investments here and the money they spend on military developments in our region overall, lending itself to the fact nobody is bold enough to say 'boo' to them over a billion dollars.

Ian McLachlan, Robert Ray, Robert Hill and other Defence Ministers, just prior and since, and their advisers, all of whom were decidedly aware of our initial mistake in the cooperation with Malaysia and the 'sunk' OPV, still hoped the deal would go hand in hand with the helicopter contract, which happened to be signed off prior to the 'Offshore Patrol Vessel' deal being confirmed; hence leading to the helicopter purchase that was now a lame duck. Not that this is a major consideration since the collapse of the whole shambles confused the easily confusable. Still, for someone on the ball, it may have given us a scant window of opportunity to consider our options as to our helicopter requirements and a chance to withdraw from the whole shambles.

I must say here after viewing the defence contracts of 1997 and 1998 and the $662 million paid to Kaman Aerospace International Group (06/97) and the $220 million paid out to Transfield Pty. Lim./ Transfield MacMahon Joint Venture/ Transfield ASI Pty. Ltd./ Transfield Construction Pty. Ltd./ Transfield Defence Systems Pty. Lim./ Transfield Ship Building, AND, Tenix(previously Transfield) Defence Systems Limited / Tenix Pty. Lim./ Tenix Defence Security Services, that both governments were friendly, then obligated, to the above enterprises. Then again, so were/are many others who deal with a department that has a bottomless budget, and obviously answerable to no one.

As a type of disclaimer I would suggest the information I have submitted is taken from various sources and some of these may or may not have been completely accurate initially, nevertheless I'm sure my targets are well holed with only a few near misses. Be that as it may, the foundation of government mishandling the purchases is as solid as a rock, and I don't believe we will ever find our billion dollars now dispersed far and wide through a multitude of inexplicable occurrences beginning with a government whiteboard contract, spilling over into Howard's new administration. And now ending with the cancellation of the deal, which I believe, is a grave error of judgement.

My view: hold out until the project is completed in some form or another.

We have been hit with the biggest con only reflected by the dodgiest car sales technique known.........exasperate the buyer of the second-hand vehicle, returned due to severe mechanical problems, until the purchaser throws up their hands in despair and informs the dealer to 'stick it where the sun doesn't shine', before driving off in their 'lemon'.

GLOSSARY

Some of you may be familiar with the following slang: for those who aren't you should find them amusing; while I'm here, and for those who have served, I will explain my reasoning in not having used naval epithets in the book. It's simple really: the people would be too easily identifiable.

BACON	CRISPY
BAILEY	BEETLES OR PEARL
BELL	DINGER OR DAISY
BENNETT	WIGGY
BRAY	DONKEY
BROWN	BOMBER
CASSIDY	HOPALONG
CLARKE	NOBBY
CRABB	BUSTER
DAVEY	JACK
DAY	DORIS
DONALD	DUCKY
FORD	HENRY
GALE	WINDY
GORDON	FLASH
GRANT	GENERAL
GRAY	DOLLY
HAYES	GABBY
HIGGINS	HENRY

HILL	WINDY
HOGAN	BEN OR HEC
HOLMES	SHERLOCK
HUDSON	ROCK
JAMES	JESSE
JONES	SPIKE OR CASEY
KELLY	NED
KENNEDY	CRASH
KERR	PEGGY
KIRBY	RIP
LANE	SHADY OR LOIS
LEACH, LEECH	BUCK
LEE	DIXIE
LEWINSKI	MONICA
LIVINGSTONE	DOC
MARSH	SWAMPY
MARTIN	PINCHER
MILLER	DUSTY
MILLS	TIMBER
MOORE	PONY
MUNRO	DARBY OR MARILYN
MURPHY	SPUD
O'NEILL	PEGGY
OAKLEY	ANNIE
PARKER	NOSEY
PATTERSON	BANJO
PAYNE	WHACKER
PERKINS	POLLY
RAY	MANTA OR STING
REED, READ	PRICKY
REYNOLDS	DEBBIE
RHODES	DUSTY
ROGERS	BUCK
RYAN	BUCK
SMITH	SMOUCH
SNOW	FROSTY

STEEL, STEELE............ RUSTY OR STAINLESS
TAYLOR .... SQUIZZY
TURNER........................ TOPSY
WATERS........................ MUDDY
WATSON........................ DOC
WHITE........................... KNOCKER
WILLIAMS.................... BUNGY
WILSON........................ TUG
WINTERS .... SHELLY
WITHERS .... GOOGIE
WOOD .... TIMBER
WOODS .... SLINGER
WRIGHT........................ SHINER

Nicknames like BLUE AND RANGA (redheads).
BONES (skinny bloke and sickbay attendants).
BULLWINKLE AND BRU (Bruhwiller).
CURLY (curly and/or a straight haired bloke).
DUTCHY (Dutch name or extraction).
LOFTY (tall bloke).
SHORTY (short arse).
PADDY (Irish).
SCOTTY (Scottish).
SLIM AND SPLINTER (skinny and tall).
TUBBY (fat and usually short).

The following is slang for colloquial navy-speak:

Arpie (RP) – Pussers radar plotter.

Bang-box – The gun turret (on big ships).

Bang – To have sex, (usually with a woman who is too drunk to confirm it).

Bangers & mash – Sausages & mashed potato.

Banyan – A sometimes impromptu beach party with a barbie and a perhaps a can or two.

Beagle Butler – Steward, Captains steward.

Belay – To cease doing something.

Birdie – Fleet Air Arm sailor(s).

Bite – To fool somebody into doing or believing something stupid.

Blue Orchid>Air Force – (RAAF) person / male or female.

Bonedome Head – usually bald.

Bones-Generally the Sick Bay Tiffy – sometimes the doctor.

Bones – Mah jongg tiles.

BR – A book of Reference or ANY book.

Brew – A cup of tea or coffee.

Buggie – Dirty or unclean person or area - eg scran bag or buggie area.

Bumnuts – Boiled eggs or just eggs.

Burgoo – Porridge (rolled oats).

Bunting tosser – Signaller, any rank.

Buzz – A rumour, sometimes true though usually not.

CDF – Common Dog Fuck (Common sense).

Chippy – The ships carpenter, also a Naval Shipwright.

Chop-chop – Move yer arse, go quickly.

Civvies – Civilian clothes or Civilian people.

Club swinger – PTI (Physical training instructor).

Cockie – Cockroach.

Corned dog – Corned beef.

Crash – Go to sleep.

Crusher – Naval patrolman.

Derps – Underwear / see also U-derps.

Dhoby – To have a wash/shower or to wash your clothes (Indian language).

Dhoby dust – Washing powder.

Dib dab – A seaman branch sailor / see also dibbie.

Dibbie-Dib dab – a seaman branch sailor.

Dig out – To make an all out effort.

Dip out – To miss out on something: to dip out.

Dit – A book or a good story to read.

Dockyard job – A big job or a major operation.

Dog watch – Two 2 hour watches to equalise the roster, also a derogatory term for a short length of service.

Doofer – A bit that goes on something, eg 'Pass the doofer' while pointing at the object, nut, washer, etc.

Duff – Refers to sticky pudding or any sweet.

Duffed – Pregnant.

Fang Tooth – or to eat /see also Yaffle.

Fang Bosun – Dentist.

Fang Farrier – Dentist.

Fart sack – Bed, bunk or hammock.

Fighting Irons – Knife, fork and spoon.

Flag waver – Signaller, any rank.

Flakers – Tired out.

Flat – Open space between mess decks on board ship, ie canteen flat.

Float test – The final test for equipment which is unserviceable.

Flunky – Officers steward (probably the most hated job).

Food fucker – Navy cook see also Tucker fucker.

Foo Foo – Pussers foot powder or Baby powder.

Four by Four – Pussers toilet paper.

Fruit salad – Multiple medal ribbons worn together.

Gash – Rubbish.

Gash hand – One who is left over after the working party has been detailed off.

Gen – The truth (genuine).

Gettas – Thongs usually illegal to wear onboard ship.

Gippers – Electrical current (ouch) or sauce or gravy.

Goddam – An American or Yank.

Goffers – Cold fizzy drinks, a big wave.

Gong – Term for medals or decorations.

Goofers – Spectators looking at something.

Green – Naive, gullible, not very knowledgeable.

Green rub – Rotten job/duty etc.

Greenie – Pussers electrical branch member.

Greenie – A large wave breaking over the ship.

Grey funnel line – Ships of the Royal Australian Navy.

Grip – A smallish bag with two carrying handles.

Hammock stower – Large overweight female.

Harpie – Girlfriend, a bit on the side, the missus - multiple meanings.

Have a wet – To have a drink.

Heads – Toilets, from the old sailing ships where the toilets were directly beneath the figure head.

Herrings in – Kippers or Herrings in tomato sauce (pronounced 'herrins in').

Hong Kong BR – A small Porno book purchased in Honkers.

Honkers – Hong Kong.

Hooker or Hook – Leading Sailor (Kellick).

Housewife – Personal sewing kit.

JarHead – A Marine - usually a US Marine.

Jaw Bosun / Jawman – See Nutman-gay-poof-pillow biter-shirt lifter.

Jimmy – First Lieutenant, XO or Number 1.

Jimmy Rick – "One-character" tile in Mah Jong.

Jockstrap – Sporty type / person.

Jong – Term for the Chinese game of Mah Jong.

Jonty or Jaunty – Master at Arms.

Kip – Short sleep or nap.

Kit muster – A personal kit inspection, also describes being sick.

Lid – Junior or Senior Sailor's cap.

Load – Sexually Transmitted Disease.

Loafing – Hanging around aimlessly, Dawdling along.

Maccas – (then)Lollies.

Maccas – (today)MacChuckburgers.

Macca Muncher – Somebody who likes lollies or sweets.

Make and mend – Early finish afternoons /usually for some special occasion, also called a 'makers'.

Make & mend sticks – Golf clubs.

Mickey Mouse – Refers to any kellick(leading seaman) or PO(petty officer) without a good conduct badge (under 4 years).

MOBI/Naval Apprentice – (Most Objectionable Bastards Imaginable).

Monkey Spunk – Vegemite

MUPPET – Naval Apprentice (Most Useless Pricks Pussers Ever Trained).

Mystery Bag – Meat pie or a sausage.

Noisy Blue – Blue-handled ratchet screwdriver.

Nosh – To eat, food, mainly a term used by the RN.

Nutman – A 'horses hoof' so to speak.

Oggie – Cornish pastie see also 'Tiddly Oggie'.

Oggin – The sea or any stretch of water.

Oppo, Stepping Oppo – Friend, Buddy, Running mate.

Outside – Life after leaving the Navy.

Party – Girlfriend.

Pavement pizza – Vomit.

Pen-pusher – Writer.

Pig / Grunter – Naval Officer.

Piglets – Midshipmen.

Pig sty – Officers Mess.

Pill pusher – The ships' Doctor.

Pinged – To be spotted from a great distance, to be picked for a particularly dirty job.

Pipe – Used on ships in place of the bugle, also the tannoy system on board ship.

Piss paddling – Barefoot - i.e. no thongs or sandals.

Piss strainers – Sautéed kidney (with bacon for breakfast).

Pit – Bed, bunk or hammock.

Plastic eggs – Pussers fried eggs (usually overdone).

Pongo – Anyone from the Army, Where the army goes the 'pong' goes.

Pope John steak – Battered fish (every Friday for lunch).

Pork Sword – Part of male anatomy, also known as beef bayonet, luncheon truncheon and pink oboe.

Pussers – The Royal Australian Navy.

Pussers hard – Pussers soap.

Rabbits – Presents or souvenirs, unofficial jobs carried out by vehicle mechanics on civvie cars.

Rack – Bunk, bed or hammock.

Rawbone – Recruit.

Redders – Tomato sauce.

Red dick – The Greenies favourite red-handled 10" screwdriver.

Red dicks – Frankfurters.

RN Dhoby – Using foo-foo instead of having a shower.

RN Sauce / RNers – Worcestershire sauce.

RN Steak – Liver or lambs fry.

Rockers – The Woolloomooloo Bay Hotel (Rock 'n Roll Hotel) - now quite upmarket.

Roughers – Stormy weather.

Run Ashore – To go out for a few 'quiet' drinks, a night out.

Sack – Fart sack, bunk, bed or hammock.

Sad on – To be unhappy or pissed off.

Scrambled Egg – Gold braid on caps of CMDR and above

Scran-Food or a meal.

Scran bag – A scruffy individual who looks like his clothes have never been ironed.

Scran bag – Also a collection point for loose bits of kit on a ship - a small fine is paid before retrieval.

Scads – Lots or a long time/ see also Yonks.

Screws – Ships propellers.

Scribe – Writer.

Scrub 'round it – To veto something or to forget it.

Sea daddy – An experienced Sailor who looks after a younger recruit to show him the ropes.

Secure – To finish for the day or after a watch.

Shiny arse – A clerk or writer.

Shirt lifter – A person on 'the other side' - see nutman.

Shiters – Drunk (pronounced 'shy-ters').

Sin bosun – Padre.

Singers – Singapore.

Sippers – A sip of a drink.

Skimmer – Surface Sailor (submariners terminology).

Slops – Naval clothing stores or clothing purchased from stores.

Snags – Sausages.

Snotty – Midshipman.

Squarie – Your regular (serious) girlfriend.

Standeasy – A break taken during the morning and the afternoon.

Starvo – Naval victualler.

Steamie / Stoker – Pussers engineering branch person.

Storm stick – Umbrella.

Suckhole – To crawl to another.

Swatties – Army personnel - see also pongo.

Technicolor yawn – Vomit.

Three badger – A Sailor with 3 good conduct stripes, (12 years undetected crime).

Tiddlygear – Nonstandard clothes usually purchased at Sinbad's, Red Anchor or Glendennings.

Tiddly Oggie – Cornish pastie see also 'Oggie.

Tiffy – Artificer.

Train smash – Tinned tomato with bacon, onion & cheese (Tomato au Gratin).

Tucker fucker – Navy cook.

Uckers – A game loosely based on ludo, probably caused more fights than almost anything else.

U-derps or Derps – Underwear.

Up the duff – Pregnant.

Wanchai burberry – Colourful Asian cane umbrella.

Ward room – Officers mess on board ship as well as in a shore establishment.

Worms in redlead – Spaghetti in tomato sauce.

Wooly pully – The thick issue jumper.

Yaffle – To eat.

Yaffling irons – Knife, fork and spoon.

Yellow peril – Smoked Haddock.

Yippee beans – Baked beans - also known in some circles as blurters (beanz meanz fartz).

Yomp – To force march with a heavy load.

Yonks – A long time.

Zap – To shoot something, or an electric shock.

Zeds – To get some sleep.

Zulu – Greenwich meantime.

1 bagger verses a 2 bagger – an ugly woman wears 1 bag so you don't have to look at her – a really ugly woman is when *you* wear a bag as well in case hers falls off. Not P.C. I know, but that's the way it was then.

*A naval *watch* is the term dealing with the watches sailors undertake on any ship. The last dog watch is the second last watch of the day broken into two watches, *dog watch* and *last dog watch*. As all other watches are four hours in duration, the dog is only two thanks to the evening meal falling between this watch. So it was shortened from the dodge watch (dodging the meal) to the dog watch. Make sense? Anyway, this is *my* last dog watch as I am nearing the end of my days; the very last watch of the day is the *evening* watch, or first watch--this is correct I think, although a little confusing too--followed by the *mid watch,* the *morning watch, forenoon* and *afternoon watch,* then the *first dog:* seven watches.

Advocate: one who acts on behalf of ex-service personnel when they seek recognition for grievances sustained during their service.

Labor Party is the correct spelling, yet while 'labour' is the correct English, the Australian Labor party has opted for the United States spelling: I'm unable to explain why.

Whiteboard allocation of funds initially came to light when Ros Kelly, the Sports Minister under Paul Keating, used a whiteboard to distribute funds to sporting organizations without actually verifying where the money was going.
I have used artistic licence here in comparing the manner in which the Seasprite contracts were initiated to those of the sporting minister.

ACKNOWLEDGEMENTS

I would like to thank Google for its wealth of information as it reintroduced me to the many aspects regarding the workings of the ships on which I served.

The Australian War Memorial whose help I sort in regard to the H.M.A.S. Sydney 3.

The Vietnam Veterans Association of Australia.

The Navy News Publications who only wanted a mention insofar as the photographs and articles I spent hours sorting through. They were extracted from their newspaper from the period 1968 through to 1975. Some photos I have used are in the public domain but I could not locate their owners. I will acknowledge them if they would like to contact me.

Thanks to whoever listed the 'pussers slang' vocabulary: their translation from navy-speak to English was, to say the least, refreshing.

Thanks to the Department of Veterans Affairs for their approval to use their article on the Vung Tau Ferry.

To my mates who know who I am and still choose to call me mate.

If I have missed anybody please let me know and I will most certainly acknowledge you in any forthcoming edition and/or articles extracted from the book.

A QUESTIONNAIRE

Please DISREGARD the following if you are so inclined, or:

I have compiled a generalised questionnaire from many sources over a period of time, including military beneficiaries, relating to compensation matters. You may want to peruse these if you are having any issues whatsoever originating from your military service.

These questions are a guide only and should *not* be regarded in any way as an unconditional diagnosis or prognosis as to your wellbeing.

I have found that self-medicating with drugs, both legal and illegal, tobacco and alcohol is common until your body no longer responds to these conventional suppressors. When that happens it may be too late as you approach your senior years; therefore as a consequence it would be advisable to consult professionals sooner rather than later.

I should also say here these questions are not only aimed at ex-service members: serving personnel and civilians alike should seek medical advice if any of the questions I have asked ring alarm bells.

DO NOT be ashamed or feel you are being a 'whinger' by seeking professional help.

Use the spaces provided if you wish to answer any of the questions.

Do you drink alcoholic beverages every day?...............
How many?........

Do you smoke?...............
How many per day?........

Do you take non-legal substances for medicinal purposes?.........

If so, what are they, why do you take them and how often?.........

Are you taking prescription medication?.........

If so, what medication do you take and what do you take it for?.........

Do you take non-prescription medication?..........

If so, what are you taking and how often do you take it?.................

Is sleeping an issue for you?...........
ie: Is your sleep regularly interrupted, do you have nightmares etc?..........
If so, please detail.........

Do you have urinating problems?........
If so, explain............

Do you have stomach upsets, irritation, gastric reflux, cramping etc?...........
Explain..........
Do you have bowel problems?..........
If so, explain (ie: Irritable Bowel Syndrome, discolouration, blood, haemorrhoids, Diverticulitis etc)...............

Have you had any intestinal operations minor and/or major including haemorrhoids?........

If so, please detail......

Do you have neck, back, hip and/or leg problems?.........

If so, explain........

Do you have heart and/or lung problems?..........

If so, please explain........

Are you often fatigued?..............

Do you have hot flushes?.........

Are you often bad-tempered?.........

Do you shy away from the general public and/or groups of people, parties, etc?.........

Are you intolerant towards your family and/or friends and/or strangers?...................

Are you violent?.........

If so when, how often and why?.........

Do you have phobias? (ie: are you afraid of confined spaces? are you afraid of crowds? are you afraid of heights, are you afraid of the dark? are you afraid of choking at ANY time and/or are you afraid of swallowing at times, whether you are eating of not? etc).........

If so, explain........

Do you have panic/anxiety attacks?...........

If so, what do they entail?...........

Do you have poor eyesight?..........

Do you have skin problems?........

If so, please explain...............

Do you have poor hearing ie: ringing in the ears? (tinnitus)? deafness? an inability to hear and/or distinguish voices in a group situation etc?..........

If so, explain..............

Have you been terminated from your employment?..........
If so, when and why?..............

And what is your current employment status?..........

If you are self-employed is this due to your inability to cope with being an employee, and/or your aversion to making a commitment to others, and/or avoiding people in general?..........

Please explain............

Have you had any broken relationships and/or marriages?........

If so, how many?..............

Do you have ANY other health issues not already covered in this questionnaire?..........
eg: Obsessive Compulsive Disorders (OCD) and depression:

Do you have gloomy thoughts as to why you are here?........

Do you feel as though your contribution to life has diminished?........

Explain how and why?......

Please do not feel your life is completely out of control if you have answered in the affirmative to some of the previous questions.

There is help, and the help you seek from your family GP and caring psychoanalysts', with the support of friends, family and community organizations all will provide you with a new lease on a life you will continue to embrace and cherish.

What I can advise you of is this: sit down and write/type your story. It is a cathartic exercise that *may* just purge you of a few demons.

My best wishes to you all.
Mark B.

A matter of life, and death.

The innocence of life in the late fifties and early sixties, forty miles west of Sydney, was so profoundly different to the world of today that we could have been foraging out an existence a hundred years ago, not fifty.

The roads were unsealed and covered by a consistent fine, red dust permeating everything in summer and turning to thick mud during the wet, nevertheless, the land was wholesome and green most of the time. The plums, passionfruit and blackberries, vine tomatoes and an assortment of other wildly growing fruits hung, glistened and untouched by the chemicals and other pollutants we have today.

Meandering through our ample back yard we enjoyed a fresh water creek clean enough in which to bath and to drink from its sandstone filtered springs. And yes, we had substantial yards on which our homes were built and where some still stand to this day; the land now subdivided and our creek desecrated to allow for further development, no doubt.

The yabbies were plentiful, along with eels and an assortment of other freshwater life; even the odd platypus. Fancy a prehistoric mammal being there in the wild with us, living in harmony: instinctively, we knew we had to respect these wondrous creatures.

We explored in bare feet, trod on wild snakes, ant nests, cow patties and numerous other wild fauna and flora, in pursuit of bush rats and rabbit. Armed with air guns and the odd .22 rifle powered by a cartridge of rat shot, we cleared areas of vermin, all in the name of good sport. All the while convincing ourselves we were doing a good thing for the environment. That is, if we considered our fragile world at all.

We had dogs and cats, who we considered our best friends, and we were convinced they would lay down their life for us at any given moment, and sometimes they did.

My future father-in-law had an English springer spaniel who, at his command, dropped flat onto a deadly brown snake when he raised his shotgun to shoot the family's supper. The dog died as it had lived, obedient and faithful. It had known the snake was there; his master didn't.

We whistled and our dogs would bound across a not-too-busy road and a couple of times they died under the odd car; they too remained forever obedient.

With my airgun I would hunt cicada with my cat and dog at my side. I would take aim and shoot, the large insect would fall and the cat would feast while the dog leaped about in hysterics, or so it seemed at the time.

I once shot a dove in an attempt at a long-range act of bravado in front of my mates. Unfortunately I hit her through the eye. She lived for a week in comfort after she had passed the lead pellet, then suddenly died in my dad's hand. I had never seen my father cry with such intensity before, or since.

As for our own vulnerabilities, crushed cars and motorbikes were on display for all to see at the local service stations, which more often than not had their own tow trucks. There were accidents where our teen brothers and sisters died violent and tragic deaths in unsafe vehicles without seat belts. Crash helmets for motorcycle riders were an option; not mandated and not worn. The remnants were there for all to see and to remind us how assailable we were.

Some lowered their cars by putting bricks in the boot because it looked cool at that time, but these bricks became missiles in collisions, usually causing more carnage than necessary.

We survived regardless, then some weren't as lucky, and some later died in faraway lands, or at the hands of cowards who would eventually bring steel-capped boots and knives to a fistfight.

We swam in dams and creeks. I drowned and was revived, and I survived a cyclone at eleven years of age. I was sucked out of my rubber rain boots and spat out into thick mud a couple of hundred feet from where I was picked up. I beheld myself in the mud from high above, although I didn't know at the time I was supposed to be dead. I was just lucky to survive, with a little help from an angel I suspect. Afterwards I had to be soaked in a bath for hours, to not only calm me, but also to dissolve the mud that had found its way into every orifice. Atonement without a scratch, and one of the many bullets I was to dodge as the years rolled out its many trials and tribulations.

As young teens the cops were there to harass us with a kick in the behind if we were in the wrong place at the wrong time. Especially after a double feature and an ongoing Batman serial at the local pictures, all for two and six, that included the movies, refreshments and maybe a shared pack of smokes. You see, the shops closed at lunchtime on Saturdays and didn't reopen until Monday morning, then if we were caught loitering where we shouldn't out would come a well-aimed police boot before we found ourselves in real trouble.

The summers were hot and the winters cold in an innocent land where we walked or rode bikes for miles and miles to anywhere and nowhere. We peddled to our schools where milk was supplied free and our religious teachers were fair and just, although they were liberal with the strap or cane with a resolve to turn us out into the world as men by the age of sixteen. Our teachers were mostly ethical and honourable, as were out dads, but they too could be bullies much like their dads before them. They were hard men who didn't hesitate to give us a clip over the ear occasionally for our wilful ways, and yet they too were mostly fair and just with a resolve to turn us out into the world as men by the age of, not sixteen, but much earlier, just as many of them had been.

Once, my dog attacked my dad when he raised his arm to give me a whack for some minor infringement to the law of his home. The dog disappeared for two days fearful of my father's wrath, but when my dad realised, and then acknowledged my ability to form such a close ally, he considered me in a new light. My dog's loyalty was unequivocal and he died before his time under the wheels of an old car as he dashed across its path.

Mums were our comfort zone, our wisdom, and our sanctuary.

We all lived and played, and our parents worked side by side within a population who were, a generation prior and in some instances, killing each other on the battlefield.

Some displayed their concentration camp forearm tattoos like badges of honour, and some carried their agony to the grave, still all got on with life.

Sure, we had ethnic differences, which were all played out in a simplistic dance of defiance with chest beating and vociferous arm waving. The occasional punch up was just a punch up without steel-toed boots and knives that cowards now bring to fist fights.

The death of a friend and family man long ago sees the changes now upon us: a survivor of war, life and teen incidents, only to be snuffed out by a coward in a fistfight who had a knife. This is my agony, my enigma.

On the lighter side of life we made fun of the 'dunny' carters. Those brave men who wore coveralls and denim berets as they lifted our toilet cans onto their broad shoulders and carried them off to their truck: each can having a little latched cabinet of its own.

We would call the trucks the fastest in the world because they had a hundred 'piss-tins'. I also recall the urban legend of the carter who dropped a full can over his raincoat hanging off the side of his truck, and when the dogged fellow went to retrieve it he was told to leave it, moreover, the company would buy him another. He replied:

"Bugger that, I'm getting my lunch out of the pocket."

When I see people wearing those little berets now I can't help but laugh out loud.

And sex was made fun of and giggled about too, yet no matter which way you looked at it all, sex was just that, sex. It's funny now though, kids regard many things sexual as not actually having sex at all. It seems peculiar to me how you can catch a sexually transmitted disease when not *really* having sex. We parents do have a lot to answer for, don't we?

Venereal diseases were almost non-existent. I'm not a moralist or prude, consequently though, promiscuity and the plagues it has brought upon us is, I assure you, no coincidence. The outcome of unwanted pregnancies then was different than the choices now available in an uncaring world where life is cheap.

Now I pass the ball to new generations as my life fades.

Life remembers everything, although we may not.

In death we see life as never before, and never again.

I just couldn't resist adding this story into my memoir after re-reading my encounter with the Reaper and the gatekeeper while serving my time on patrol boats in Chapter 5.

While not exactly in line with the prose of the book itself (I had actually met Stuart as described earlier while still serving), I decided to write the following yarn for a short story horror website using the same characters as I encountered way back when. I may add that all the persons living and dead in the story were actual people, as was the bar, the barkeeper, the hospital and morgue, my friend, my deceased friends, the nurse I later encountered, along with the decadent drunk; yet it remains to be seen who is still out there.

The following is a true account of what occurred: as true as I am sitting here, although some non-persons may or may not have existed.

I will leave it up to you to decide.

A WALK WITH THE REAPER

"Fear of death is worse than death itself"
William Shakespeare

I had met Stuart quite by accident one bitter, stormy night a few decades ago now, while on a drinking binge in a freezing inner Sydney winter. He was alone at the end of a lonely bar, yet he was warm and friendly in keeping with the mood of the premises itself. He then nodded and the smile stayed, as did mine along with the barkeep.

I ordered a beer with a rum chaser just to ease the burden of the cold, which had been my excuse after my most recent relationship collapsed, leaving me heartbroken and bitter at the world.

I had finally given my heart to a young woman after years of frivolous behaviour and asked her to marry me, only to later discover she was having an affair with her college professor. Still, I didn't wish her well as they embarked on an interstate love affair that eventually crashed, as these flings with higher male educators often do.

A fire softly crackled in the corner a few metres from an old jukebox where my new friend was perched absorbing the warmth, while I took in the old timber panelling that decorated every wall, along with the solid aged and pitted redwood bar. A few booths occupied by no one, on seats badly in need of repair, meandered along one wall. The decorations consisted of old sports memorabilia by way of photos and a few banners, as well as portraits of old movie stars now dead and buried, nevertheless not yet forgotten by my generation.

I wandered over to the jukebox to glean a little warmth and to listen to an old Kenny Rogers song playing sarcastically, *'You picked a fine time to leave me Lucille'*. Terrific, I thought, just the song to send me off again, when my new friend turned to me and said:

"Pretty shitty song, hey?"

"You can take that to the bank, for sure," I replied, then offered a hand, "I'm Alban, by the way."

"Stuart," was he all said and extended a hand to me, which I gratefully accepted. His grip was firm and warm, yet a little calloused, although the skin was soft between the hard tissue. I returned his solid welcome in the same manner, unlike some limp-wristed weasels one meets from time to time:

"Can I buy you one mate?"

"Sure," I said.

"Beer and rum again."

"Got it in one, thanks."

With that he pulled out a wad of notes and counted what looked to be the right amount of money for his drink as well.

"What are you having there?" I asked

"Just a whiskey for the road."

"Off home are you?" I said.

"No. To work."

"Fuck, you must have a good job. Are you a wharfie?" was all I could splutter.

He just smiled at me and said he was a Coroner's assistant, and this midnight shift was the gatekeeper's watch at the city morgue, a couple of blocks away in a back street behind the old hospital.

I guess we would refer to it as the graveyard shift: an apt name I believe.

"Just helps me get through the night is all," he said.

"Don't blame you mate. So what is it you do exactly, especially at this time of night?" I asked.

"Take care of the clients as they arrive, then wait for their next of kin to come and identify them."

As we drank we conversed about the living and the dead for a short time until he said it was time for him to go.

"Can I buy you one for the road Stuart?"

"No thanks Alban, and call me Stu, ok." It was not a question, and he got my name first up, which surprised me.

"Sure Stu, call me Al, some call me Big Al, but as you can see I'm not that big, now."

"Alban was a Christian martyr, wasn't he?"

"Yeah, third century, first Christian martyr slain on British soil. Made him a saint my folks told me years ago, never had much time for Pommies myself though: must be something in that," I said, smiling.

"Ok Al. See you here tomorrow night bout elevenish and I'll take you for a tour through the morgue."

He was not really asking me, and he wasn't really telling me, if you know what I mean.

After I had regained my footing having nearly choked on my rum, I said:

"Sure, why not, I've got nothing else on, so why not a visit to the other side. Besides, I always shout my way back into the bar and this bar is no exception. I still own you one Stu."

I followed him out and as I turned to bid farewell to the barman I felt a rush of freezing air hit me in the back as my friend left us. I quickly followed buttoning my old navy coat against the chill that quickly pervaded my whole being, at the same time lifting my arm to wave to Stu, only to find he had gone: gone in a couple of seconds, or what seemed to be milliseconds. I looked up and down the forlorn, narrow street left unchanged from its inception decades earlier, yet retaining a sense of being dragged reluctantly into the late twentieth century.

I wandered the cold and lonely back streets to my two-room inner city flatette: modest digs in a world not known for its modesty. My life was at a crossroads, my squandered years in the navy, my equally squandered education and childhood, and an ability to fall in love too quickly usually ending in a fruitless volley of hate and tears.

My job was just that, a job, in a 'walk over dead bodies' to gain an advantage in the never ending conflagration known as the public service. I was gladly left behind in a position no one cared about, including me. I robotically ploughed through paperwork of no consequence and then robotically held out my hand every fortnight for a meagre pay packet that just kept me going on booze and cigarettes with the occasional joint to keep me company and ease a self-inflicted pain.

In bed that night I wondered about my new found friend and the work and life to which he had committed himself. While he had disclosed a somewhat vague reassurance that he was happy doing what he was doing I had an uneasy feeling there was going to be more to his story. With that thought I slept a sleep of the dead until my annoying alarm sounded its death knell for another day of dreaded brain-numbing work.

I stumbled into the bar around ten the following evening to find myself, Stu and the barman the only three in the place again, although still warm and friendly as was the previous night, but my condition a little more weathered not only to fight off the cold but also to fight off the fear of venturing into the unknown.

I bought Stu a whisky neat as was his poison then sobered up almost immediately when he said it was all a go for this evening with no deaths due to violent abuse, accidents and the like: he had called from the bar moments before I arrived to enquire as to the situation.

"Well that's a relief, I think. Only for the sake of possible victims maybe not having to present themselves for cold room accommodation this evening," I said.

That notwithstanding, the notion I may be spared the horror of staring death in the face, which I didn't care to mention to him there and then, was somewhat reassuring.

We moderately drank until close to midnight, then grabbed our coats and left the comfort of the bar while farewelling the keep, whose name I cannot recall to this day: something that rhymed with something........

Why is it that all these 'well beyond their use by date' hospitals had a back street with a dark and gloomy entrance to accommodate the dead, I thought? Just like in the old horror movies. There wasn't a soul to be seen, but it occurred to me there and then that no one would hang around a morgue, would they, ever?

The cold ripped through us, through me anyway, since Stu didn't seem to flinch at the churlish winter. I didn't think much of it at the time; I considered he may be used to it and had become immune to low temperatures working in a cold storage facility.

I reluctantly followed him into the dimly lit passage, up a few steps and into a well-maintained lounge area. In fact, it left my humble abode for dead, with its fully equipped kitchen that even had the newish scary invention, a top of the range microwave oven. The carpeted lounge area had all the mod cons with luxury sofa, good sound system and television. A bunk bed and bathroom strayed off to the side of the relaxation room so one could sleep and shower. He explained that he could nap if things were quiet and be paid an exorbitant amount of money while doing so.

"No one wants to do this job Al. No one wants to go home to his family smelling of death. It's a job for a single bloke who has no family or friends to answer to or rely on," he explained.

He then went to the fridge, grabbed a beer, pushed it into my hand and continued with his colloquy.

"I took on this job a couple of years back after my wife and little girl were killed in a car accident, on a night much the same as this. Shit weather, shit road, shit drunk ran right over the top of 'em in a truck. I was at work bowing before the gaffer to get ahead keeping his fuckin' books for him. They wouldn't have had to come out and get me from my shit job if I hadn't been kissing the arse of a fat fuck who had no concern at all for the people who kissed his fuckin' feet every day. I should have knocked off at five and caught a bus home like normal people do."

"I resigned," he continued. "After I told him to jam it where the sun don't shine, sold up everything and nearly drank myself to death. So then along comes this bloke I met at the same bar we met at last night, who tells me they're looking for a solid type of bloke to take over the late shift at the morgue here. I said to him fuck that, and then thought why not; after all it's the same morgue where I had to identify my beautiful wife and daughter, although they weren't beautiful anymore especially after I had to identify them, or what was left of them."

"Woo-oh there Stu," I said. "You are working in the same place where they brought your family?"

"Why not? I feel close to them here, and I can feel the grief of the loved ones the new ones leave behind who have to come here to identify them. My only friend is the Coroner because he sees in me a caring lost soul, I think. We work well together and he even supplied me with the most expensive set of autopsy tools."

I shuddered and grabbed another beer, then said:

"Who the hell was this bloke who asked you to step into this job, and where did the previous keeper go?"

"Oh, he overdosed on booze and medication, this old guy told me. He said I should go around to the office here and apply, so I did. When I asked the Coroner interviewing me who the old fart I spoke to was, he just shrugged his shoulders and said he didn't know."

"Fuck," I lamented.

He went on in a droning type of voice:

"So here I am, sober, sort of, and on a mild type of medication the Coroner provides me with to help me get through the tough ones."

"The tough ones?"

"Yeah, you know. The little children who are bought in here after being beaten to death by fucked out, brain dead parents who should have been neutered at birth. And autopsies have to be done on all of them to determine how they actually died so we can gaol the fuckers who killed 'em. That's not to mention the kids killed in accidents, like cars and such. As a matter of fact we have a toddled here now in the fridge that I will be operating on first thing in the morning, with the Coroner of course. I'll show you later; just wanted to warn you first. We have unidentified poor bastards too who died out there on the streets and we just keep 'em in cold storage until someone comes along to identify and claim them."

"And what if no one comes in to claim them?" I ventured.

"We have a special place to keep 'em, forever if necessary. I'll show where, later. We also have a very special room to accommodate murder victims and those who die under suspicious circumstances; that too on the tour."

Funny though, I recall how I felt comfortable with all this now. It may have been the alcohol or it may have been his voice that calmed me; it may have been my need to be somewhere else in this life. So far, my existence had been a waste. Maybe Stu was looking for a replacement, a sidekick, or just a friend. I found him both interesting and trustworthy; his honesty and integrity may have also been a factor.

Time rolled by and in the blink of an eye it struck three a.m. when my host said it was time for a wander through the house of horrors.

"This way," he said, and with that we walked along a sparse narrow corridor that opened up into a small room with a glass window looking into a chamber with a metal gurney placed strategically in the centre, on which was resting, thankfully, no body.

"This is the viewing area if the person who is identifying the deceased doesn't want to actually go inside the room itself. Now we'll just go down these few steps, watch out though, it's dark. The bloody light blows every time you go to switch it on. Can't get it fixed either."

We entered a very large clean metal and tile chamber with smaller similar rooms containing the same paraphernalia branching off from the main facility, all with metal tables, medical instruments, sinks, buckets, and drains everywhere you stepped.

While Stu was explaining the ins and outs of his workstation my eyes darted this way and that trying to take in all the nothingness around me.

Stu then said:

"This room here is for the victims of murder or suspected of meeting their demise by foul means. They all get special treatment right through to burial or cremation. Each has their own story to tell and it's a matter of finding the key to unlock their secret. This is the interesting part of the job."

"And the rest?" I asked.

"They too have a story to tell and sometimes I can hear them talking to me, especially the ones who have met a violent end. The children though, they're another story," he trailed off.

"We'll take a look in our famous cold storage room now but don't be scared. Once you meet everyone you'll feel right at home."

"Hope not." I whispered.

"You'll be ok, promise."

He then opened the door to this room of approximately twelve metres by twelve metres when a rush a freezing air hit me like a train and stopped me dead in my tracks, yet the keeper actually floated in through the threshold, or so I thought at the time. He floated back out to me and took my hand to guide me into his world, which I gratefully acknowledged while excusing myself insofar as my own credulity was concerned.

If you see modern movies or be unlucky enough to have to pay a visit to a morgue, you will probably see a completely different set up concerning the placement of the dearly departed. They each have their own cabinet or draw to lay at rest now, but this place had all the recently deceased laying side by side and head to toe on their trolleys throughout the room, along with shelves where bodies in clear plastic were nestled. Some on the trolleys were covered with the flimsiest of cloth, while recent guests where clothed, to an extent, depending on the condition of the remains.

I felt no cold whatsoever now, due to who knows what?

The first person I encountered I knew immediately from my love of football at the time. He was a young A Grader recently recruited by our own local inner city team and had been up in a roof fixing some dodgy wiring at his mother's home when he suffered an electrical mishap. They found him some hours later, owning to his being there alone at the time. He was still in his club jumper and shorts and when Stu said I should shake his hand to bid him farewell, I did as he instructed. I gently took his hand and gave it a slight lift then I let it go and that's where it stayed poised a little above the metal gurney. As I turned my back, Stu said his hand came down with so much force that it made an almighty bang, which saw me jump at least three feet. My friend's explanation was the young player, being so pissed off at his own untimely demise, that it was all he could do to show his anger, and sure enough when I turned to look the young footballer's fist was clenched and resting on his uncomfortable bed.

Holy hell, and I had only just passed go, still I felt no danger at all, just pure unadulterated fear of the unknown. Does that make sense?

The smell was overpowering I can tell you. Even to this day I won't go into a walk-in freezer where beef is stored. It's that old dead carcass smell if you know what I mean: the acrid smell of death.

This place was like a cold wax museum where all who occupied the room of death were wax-like with their features frozen in eternity at their moment of passing. None smiling, none happy in leaving us, none waving goodbye; all stateless and alone. A man with a crushed head winked at me with his only good eye, since the other had been popped clean out of his head and now lay on his crushed cheek: run over by a bus said Stu.

A tattooed woman of the streets finally met the one client who sliced her from vagina to sternum while he continued to fuck her: so said the police to Stu.

A homeless woman run down by a train in pieces wrapped in plastic on a shelf, unclaimed and unidentified, staring down at me with her foot resting on her forehead and asking, no, pleading with me to help her.

Others with all manner of injuries, or just ordinary old age finally catching up to some, yet these looked most at peace along with a small child of about one or two years of age. Did I say previously that none were smiling? I was wrong on this point. The child seemed to have a smile on his or her face. I didn't want to ask the sex of the little one who now looked to me to be somehow content. After all, the beatings and what appeared to be burn marks indicated to me of a better place, at peace here among the dead.

"Is this the kid you told me about who had been beaten to death?" I enquired.

"Sure is Al, we'll look after that one early in the morning. You may want to look in on us if you're still here and see how we go about it in the special room."

"Yeah, like that's going to happen," was my puerile reply.

179

Stu just smiled a knowing smile, which caused me to take stock of where I was, and in a fleeting instant I believed my new friend was grooming me to take over, if and when he left his position as gatekeeper of the dead.

I began to consider that a few years stint was about the distance one would be able to travel before it took its toll, and more than likely one would end up in the very same cold room keeping company with the other unfortunates.

I continued my journey looking and touching the dead and to this day I'm not really sure why; nevertheless I became aware of how we will all be here in a place like this one day no matter what your standing in life may have been. And at the end of our time we will all be equal in status, naked and dead: a sour and sobering realisation.

"Fuck me Stu, I know this bloke here too. How come he has a corner to himself?" All around him the dead talked to me. The young biker decapitated with his head carefully placed on his torso by the caring keeper; the old lady at peace after a lifetime of stories to tell; a young bullied girl who suicided as a last resort; the shooting victim and the domestic incident that left a wife beater with a large knife wound in his chest.........

"I worked with this guy about a year back when I had some paperwork to see to at a rehabilitation centre. I think he was a therapist of some kind. How come he's here separated from the rest?" I asked again.

"He died of a suspected contagious virus, so no autopsy is going to be performed. Some news drifting in from the States about a homosexual disease goin' about. He was very active with other men so it's a hands off case; we don't know what we're goin' to do with him. He's separated so no one gets confused and decides to perform an autopsy on him. It's on his toe tag as well."

I had liked this tall young man and he had indicated to me that he was well travelled. It came out later he was indeed our very first AIDS victim here in Australia after a hedonistic lifestyle, it seemed.

A bell sounded, so Stuart hurried out to attend to a new arrival after telling me to hang on a tic and that he would be back shortly.

I didn't stay though and as I stepped out of the door I turned to my hosts and made the sign of the cross, along with a short prayer for their benefit: an old Catholic blessing from my childhood aeons ago and something I had not done since I don't know when. They all went quiet; I'm positive they smiled at me.

I walked out of the morgue and into a breaking belligerent day without any goodbyes to my host, and then made my way home. I later called my work and said I was not well, but would be in the next day if I had recovered.

That evening I paid a sober visit to the bar only to be greeted by a frosty barkeep in a cold empty room. An icy shadow crossed his face when I enquired as to Stu's whereabouts, to which he replied:

"No one here by that name."

"I can see that. So what's the problem with the fire and warmth, or should I say, lack of warmth?"

"We're closed. You should go before we change our mind, my friend."

"About what?" I barked.

"Just go now," he replied with such malevolence that I was lost for words.

"Pass on a message to Stu, sport, thanks but no thanks."

"We already know that. You lost us when you left the cold room."

I shook my head, turned around and when I got to the door he said:

"Mr Stuart is no longer with us. He was, how do I say, somewhat too generous with our deceased and lax with his choice when recruiting new personnel."

"Too bad sport, your loss." I said caustically.

I walked home in a warmer climate than the one I had just left and while strolling along feeling as light as a feather it occurred to me that I may have just had an audience with the Reaper. You really had to be there, I guess. I contemplated all day and searched my inner most soul for answers. The dead had spoken to me and when

I found my faith again in that cold place it immediately eliminated me from contention to relieve Stu from his position.

He was there in some type of Purgatory doing penance for his own self-inflicted demise over the loss of his family, and working in a place of death also finally took its toll by way of medication and alcohol.

I enquired as to his whereabouts at the main hospital only to be told he had died a year previously, almost to the day. I then asked who was doing his job now.

"Just another lost soul," she smirked from behind a cloven austerity.

"Do I look like another lost soul to you." It wasn't a question.

"Not any more you don't."

And from that day forward I made it my primary objective to live a better life, one day at a time.

As for the bar: when I went back there to tell the barkeep he could stick his place where the sun doesn't shine: much the same as the place he came from, I figured, it wasn't there. Just a washed out vacant place that hadn't seen the light of day for God knows how long.

I turned to walk away only to come face to face with a filthy and decaying old drunk who sniffed me and then asked for money, which I gave over to him. He winked at me and said in a gravelled menacing voice:

"See you again some day, sport."

is vere est finis?